60 More Quick Knits

20 Hats ✳ 20 Scarves ✳ 20 Mittens in Cascade 220® Sport

sixth&spring books
NEW YORK

sixth&spring books

161 Avenue of the Americas, New York, New York 10013
sixthandspringbooks.com

Managing Editor
WENDY WILLIAMS

Senior Editor
MICHELLE BREDESON

Art Director
DIANE LAMPHRON

Instructions Editors
PAT HARSTE
STEPHANIE MRSE
AMY POLCYN

Instructions
Proofreaders
STEPHANIE MRSE
AMY POLCYN
JUDY SLOAN

Editorial Assistant
ALEXANDRA
JOINNIDES

Copy Editor
KRISTIN JONES

Technical Illustrations
ULI MONCH

Photography
JACK DEUTSCH

Stylist & Bookings
Manager
SARAH LIEBOWITZ

Hair and Makeup
ALEJANDRA

Vice President,
Publisher
TRISHA MALCOLM

Creative Director
JOE VIOR

Production Manager
DAVID JOINNIDES

President
ART JOINNIDES

Library of Congress Control Number: 2011931159
ISBN: 978-1-936096-21-3

4765 2408 1/12

Manufactured in China

1 3 5 7 9 10 8 6 4 2

First Edition

cascadeyarns.com

contents

✳ To locate retailers that carry
Cascade 220 Sport, visit cascadeyarns.com.

Bobbles and Lace Slouchy Hat

Refined and ladylike, this pretty topper will be the envy of all your girlfriends. Knit in a soft neutral, it makes a perfect accessory for early fall.

DESIGNED BY MURLA LEAHY

Size
Instructions are written for one size.

Knitted Measurements
Circumference at brim (un-stretched)
Approx 18"/45.5 cm

Materials
- 2 1¾oz/50g hanks (each approx 164yd/150m) of *Cascade 220 Sport* (Peruvian highland wool) in #8021 beige
- One each sizes 6 and 7 (4 and 4.5mm) circular needles, 16"/40cm long *or size to obtain gauge*
- One set (5) size 7 (4.5mm) double-pointed needles (dpns) *or size to obtain gauge*
- Stitch marker

Stitch Glossary
MB (make bobble) (K1, yo, k1, yo, k1) in next st, turn, p5, turn, ssk, k1, ssk. Sl second and third sts, one at a time, over first st.
S2KP Sl 2 sts as if to k2tog, k1, pass 2 sl sts over k1.

Twisted Rib
(over an even number of sts)
Rnd 1 *K1 tbl, p1; rep from * around.
Rep rnd 1 for twisted rib.

Hat
With smaller needles, cast on 104 sts. Pm and join, being careful not to twist sts. Work in twisted rib until piece measures 2"/5cm from beg, inc one st on last row—105 sts.
Change to larger needles.

BEG CHART
Rnd 1 Work 15-st rep 7 times around. Cont to work chart in this manner until rnds 1–24 have been completed twice.

CROWN SHAPING
Note Change to dpns when there are too few sts to fit comfortably on needles.
Rnd 1 *Yo, ssk, p1, ssk, k7, k2tog, p1; rep from * around—91 sts.
Rnd 2 *K2, p1, ssk, k5, k2tog, p1; rep from * around—77 sts.
Rnd 3 *K2tog, yo, p1, ssk, k3, k2tog, p1; rep from * around—63 sts.

Gauge
22 sts and 28 rnds to 4"/10cm over lace pat, using larger needle (after blocking). *Take time to check gauge.*

Bobbles and Lace Slouchy Hat

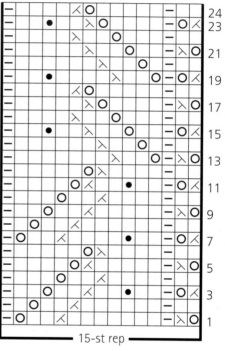

Rnd 4 *K2, p1, ssk, k1, k2tog, p1; rep from * around—49 sts.
Rnd 5 *Yo, ssk, p1, S2KP, p1; rep from * around—35 sts.
Rnd 6 *K2, p1, k1, p1; rep from * around.
Rnd 7 *K2tog; rep from * end, k1—18 sts.

Finishing
Cut yarn and thread through rem sts. Pull tight and weave in threads. To block, soak in tepid water and wool wash. Stretch over a dinner plate to dry. See notes on chart. ■

Stitch Key

☐	Knit
⊟	Purl
Ⓞ	Yo
⟋	Ssk
⟍	K2tog
⦿	MB (Make Bobble)

15-st rep

Baltic Mittens

These stunning hand-warmers feature several dazzling details, including
a beautiful all-over Fair Isle pattern with a contrasting pattern framed
by Latvian braids. The results are well worth the effort.

DESIGNED BY HEIDI TODD KOZAR

SIZE
Instructions are written for one size.

Knitted Measurements
Hand circumference 9"/23cm
Length of cuff Approx 4"/10cm

Materials
■ 1 1¾oz/50g hank (each approx
164yd/150m) of *Cascade 220 Sport*
(Peruvian highland wool) each in #9543
midnight blue (A) and #2452 turtle (B)

■ One set (5) each sizes 3 and 4
(3.25 and 3.5mm) double-pointed needles
(dpns) *or size to obtain gauge*

■ Stitch marker

Note To work in the rnd, always read
charts from right to left.

Corrugated Rib
(multiple of 4 sts)
Rnd 1 *K2 with A, k2 with B;
rep from * around.
Rep rnd 1 for corrugated rib.

Latvian Braid
Latvian braid is created by carrying
color not in use across RS of work, rather
than WS.
Rnd 1 *K1 with A, k1 with B; rep from *
around.
Rnd 2 Reel off long lengths of both
colors. Bring both colors forward to RS.
P1 with A, p1 with B, matching colors in
the rnd below. Keep colors alternating
and always bring the next color to p *over*
the last st. This will twist the yarn as you
p around the mitten.
Rnd 3 P1 with A, p1 with B, matching
colors in the rnd below. Keep colors
alternating and always bring the next
color to p *under* the last st. This will
release the twist from the yarn as you p
around the mitten.
Work rnds 1–3 for Latvian braid.

Right Mitten
CUFF
With smaller dpns and A, cast on 60 sts.
Divide sts over 4 needles (15 sts on each
needle). Join, taking care not to twist sts
on needles, pm for beg of rnds. Cont in
St st (k every rnd) for 9 rnds.
Next (picot) rnd *Yo, k2tog;
rep from * around. K next 2 rnds. Cont in
corrugated rib and work even 13 rnds.
Change to larger dpns.
Next (inc) rnd With A, k inc 4 sts evenly
spaced around—64 sts. Work rnds 1–3
of Latvian braid.
Next rnd With A, knit.
BEG CHART PAT I
Rnd 1 Work 16-st rep 4 times. Cont to
foll chart in this way to rnd 12. Work
rnds 1–3 of Latvian braid.
Next rnd With B, knit.

Gauge
28 sts and 28 rnds to 4"/10cm over chart pats using larger dpns. *Take time to check gauge.*

Baltic Mittens

HAND
BEG CHART PAT II
Rnd 1 Work 64 sts of chart. Cont to foll chart in this way to rnd 13.

THUMB PLACEMENT
Rnd 14 Work first 2 sts foll chart, k10 onto waste yarn, sl these 10 sts back to LH needle; beg with st 3 of chart, k these 10 sts again, then work to end of rnd. Cont to foll chart through rnd 33.

TOP SHAPING
Rnds 34–48 Work to top of chart, working dec as indicated—4 sts. Cut A leaving a 6"/15cm tail. Thread tail in tapestry needle, then thread through rem sts. Pull tog tightly and secure end. Cut and weave in B on WS.

THUMB
Remove waste yarn and place 20 live sts on dpns as foll: 10 sts below thumb opening on needle 2 and 10 sts above opening on needle 4.

BEG CHART PAT III
Rnd 1 With RS facing, needle 1 and A, pick up and k 2 sts along RH edge of thumb opening, k10 from needle 2; with needle 3, pick up and k 2 sts along LH edge of thumb opening; k10 from needle 4, pm for beg of rnds—24 sts. Divide sts evenly between 4 needles (6 sts on each). Cont chart on rnd 2 and work to top of chart, working dec as shown—4 sts. Cut B leaving a 6"/15cm tail. Thread tail in tapestry needle, then thread through rem sts. Pull tog tightly and secure end. Cut A and weave in end.

Left Mitten
Work same as right mitten to thumb placement.

THUMB PLACEMENT
Rnd 14 Work first 30 sts foll chart, k10 onto waste yarn, sl these 10 sts back to LH needle; beg with st 31 of chart, k these 10 sts again, then work to end of rnd. Cont to foll chart through rnd 33. Cont to work same as right mitten.

Finishing
Turn bottom edge of cuff to WS along picot rnd and hem in place. Block pieces to measurements. ■

Color Key

Midnight Blue (A)

Turtle (B)

Stitch Key
Knit

K2tog

Ssk

No stitch

CHART I

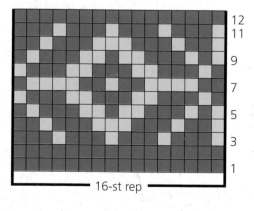

16-st rep

CHART III

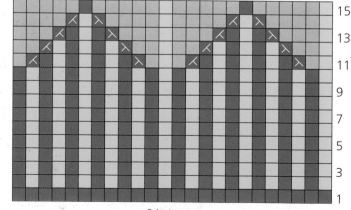

24 sts

Baltic Mittens

CHART II

64 sts

Quick Tip
When working from a Fair Isle chart, keep your place by applying
a piece of sticky paper above the row you are knitting.

Snowflake Scarf with Pompoms

Head to the skating rink or make a snow angel in this traditional winter-motif scarf.
Knitting in a tube makes the colorwork quick and easy.

DESIGNED BY YOKO HATTA

Sizes
Instructions are written for one size.

Knitted Measurements
Approx 6" x 44"/15cm x 111.5cm
(excluding pompoms)

Materials
- 4 1¾oz/50g hanks (each approx 164yd/150m) of *Cascade 220 Sport* (Peruvian highland wool) in #8401 silver grey (MC)
- 1 1¾oz/50g hank (each approx 164yd/150m) of Cascade Yarns 220 Sport (Peruvian highland wool) in #8010 natural (CC)
- One set (5) size 6 (4mm) and size 5 (3.75mm) double-pointed needles (dpns) *or size to obtain gauge*
- Stitch marker
- 3"/7.5cm pompom maker

Stitch Glossary
kf&b Inc 1 by knitting into the front and back of the next st.

Scarf
With smaller needles and MC, cast on 36 sts using a provisional method and leaving a 12"/30.5cm tail. Join and pm, taking care not to twist sts on needle.
Next rnd Kf&b around—72 sts. Work in St st (knit every rnd) for 25 rnds. Change to larger needles. Beg color chart, working 2 repeats of chart around and stranding color not in use loosely on WS of work. Cont chart for a total of 29 rnds. Cut CC, change to smaller needles. Work with MC in St st for 226 rnds. Change to larger needles and rep color chart as before for 29 rnds. Cut CC, change to smaller needles. Work with MC in St st for 25 rnds.
Next rnd K2tog around—36 sts. Cut yarn, leaving a 12"/30.5cm tail and thread through rem sts. Pull tog tightly and secure end.

Finishing
Undo provisional cast-on. Thread tail through rem sts. Pull tog tightly and secure end. Block piece lightly to measurements.

POMPOMS (MAKE 2)
Using equal amounts of both colors, wrap yarn densely around a 3"/7.5cm pompom maker. Finish pompom following package directions. Attach a pompom to each end of scarf. ■

Gauges
24 sts and 30½ rows to 4"/10cm over St st using size 5 (3.75mm) needles. 24 sts and 26 rows to 4"/10cm over stranded color pat using size 6 (4mm) needles. *Take time to check gauges.*

Fair Isle Scarf with Pompoms

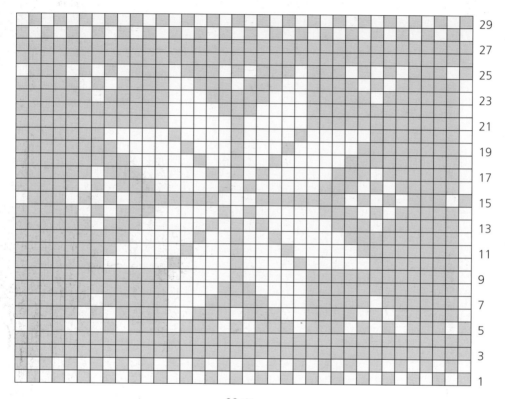

36 sts

Color Key

Silver Grey (MC)

Natural (CC)

Bull's-Eye Beret

A spot-on project for learning to knit in the round, this beret knits up quickly. Five shades of blue create a beautiful, gradated effect. A multicolored pompom tops it off.

DESIGNED BY CHERYL MURRAY

■■□□

Size
Instructions are written for one size.

Knitted Measurements
Head circumference 20"/51cm
Diameter 11"/28cm

Materials
■ 1 1¾oz/50g hank (each approx 164yd/150m) of *Cascade 220 Sport* (Peruvian highland wool) each in #8892 azure (A), #9420 como blue (B), #8891 cyan blue (C), #9421 blue hawaii (D) and #8906 blue topaz (E)

■ Size 6 (4mm) circular needle, 16"/40cm long *or size to obtain gauge*

■ One set (5) size 6 (4mm) double-pointed needles (dpns)

■ Stitch marker

■ 3"/7.5cm pompom maker

Beret
With A, cast on 92 sts. Join and pm, taking care not to twist sts on needle. Work around in k2, p2 rib for 14 rnds.
Next (inc) rnd *K2, M1; rep from * around——138 sts. Cont St st (knit every rnd) and stripe pat as foll:

With B, work for 15 rnds. With C, work for 15 rnds. With D, work for 8 rnds.

CROWN SHAPING
Change to dpns (dividing sts evenly between 4 needles) when there are too few sts on circular needle. Cont working with D as foll:
Dec rnd 1 *K10, S2KP, k10; rep from * around—126 sts. Knit next rnd.
Dec rnd 2 *K9, S2KP, k9; rep from * around—114 sts. Knit next rnd.
Dec rnd 3 *K8, S2KP, k8; rep from * around—02 sts. Knit next rnd.
Dec rnd 4 *K7, S2KP, k7; rep from * around—90 sts. Knit next rnd. Change to E.
Dec rnd 5 *K6, S2KP, k6; rep from * around—78 sts. Knit next rnd.
Dec rnd 6 *K5, S2KP, k5; rep from * around—66 sts. Knit next rnd.
Dec rnd 7 *K4, S2KP, k4; rep from * around—54 sts. Knit next rnd.
Dec rnd 8 *K3, S2KP, k3; rep from * around—42 sts. Knit next rnd.
Dec rnd 9 *K2, S2KP, k2; rep from * around—30 sts. Knit next rnd.
Dec rnd 10 *K1, S2KP, k1; rep from * around—18 sts. Knit next rnd.
Dec rnd 11 [S2KP] 6 times—6 sts.
Cut yarn leaving an 8"/20.5cm tail and thread through rem sts. Pull tog tightly and secure end.

Finishing
Stretch beret over a 12"/30.5cm-diameter dinner plate or heavy cardboard circle. Steam-block; let dry.

POMPOM
Beg with color A and, adding colors in same sequence as for beret, wrap yarn densely around a 3"/7.5cm pompom maker. Finish pompom following package directions. Sew pompom to center top of beret. ■

Gauge
22 sts and 30 rnds to 4"/10cm over St st using size 6 (4mm) circular needle. *Take time to check gauge.*

Star-Motif Mittens

Reach for the stars in these two-colored Fair Isle mittens. With a star motif and whimsical star tassels, these mittens are ideal for late night stargazing.

DESIGNED BY FIONA ELLIS

Size
Instructions are written for one size.

Knitted Measurements
Hand circumference 7¼"/18.5cm
Length of cuff Approx 2½"/6.5cm

Materials
■ 1 1¾oz/50g hank (each approx 164yd/150m) of *Cascade 220 Sport* (Peruvian highland wool) each in #9543 midnight blue (A) and #9421 blue hawaii (B)

■ One set (5) size 6 (4mm) double-pointed needles (dpns) *or size to obtain gauge*

■ Stitch markers

Notes
1) To work in the rnd, always read charts from right to left.
2) When working thumb gussets, carry B across WS of work, stranding it every 2 or 3 sts to prevent long floats.

Right Mitten
CUFF
With A, cast on 48 sts. Divide sts over 4 needles (12 sts on each). Join, taking care not to twist sts on needles, pm for beg of rnds.
Rnd 1 With A, k.
Rnd 2 With A, p.
Rnd 3 With B, sl 1 pwise wyib, *k2, sl 2 pwise wyib; rep from * around, end k2, sl 1 pwise wyib.
Rnd 4 With B, sl 1 pwise wyib, *p2, sl 2 pwise wyib; rep from * around, end p2, sl 1 pwise wyib.
Rnds 5 and 6 With A, k.
Rnd 7 With A, p. Cont in St st (k every rnd) as foll:
BEG CHART PAT I
Rnd 1 Work 4-st rep 12 times. Cont to foll chart in this way through rnd 15.

BEG CHART PAT II
Beg chart on rnd 1 and work even through rnd 2.

THUMB GUSSET
Rnd 3 Work first 23 sts of chart, [with A k in front of next st, pm, then k in back of same st] twice, work last 23 sts of chart—50 sts.
Rnd 4 Work first 24 sts of chart, sl marker, with A, k2, sl marker,
work last 24 sts of chart.
Rnd 5 Work first 24 sts of chart, sl marker, with A, M1, k to next marker, M1, sl marker, work last 24 sts of chart—52 sts. Cont to foll chart in this way through rnd 16, working inc as shown—62 sts.
Rnd 17 Work first 24 sts of chart, place 14 thumb sts on scrap yarn, work last 24 sts of chart—48 sts. Cont to work to top of chart, dec top of mitten as shown—24 sts. Using B, weave sts tog using Kitchener st or use 3-needle bind-off.

THUMB
Place 14 sts on scrap yarn on 2 dpn (7 sts on each needle). With 3rd needle and A, pick up and k 2 sts along top edge of thumb opening, pm for beg of rnds—16 sts. Divide sts over 3 needles. Cont in St st for 1½"/4cm.

TOP SHAPING
Dec rnd 1 [K2tog] 8 times—8 sts. K next rnd.
Dec rnd 2 [K2tog] 4 times—4 sts. Cut yarn leaving a 6"/15cm tail. Thread tail in tapestry needle, then thread through rem sts. Pull tog tightly and secure end.

Gauge
26 sts and 28 rnds to 4"/10cm over chart pats using size 6 (4mm) dpns. *Take time to check gauge.*

Star-Motif Mittens

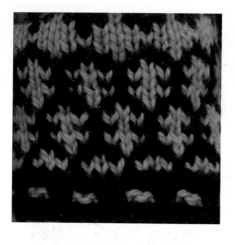

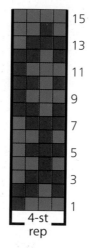

CHART I

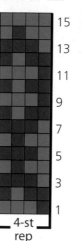

4-st rep

CHART III

15
13
11
9
7
5
3
1

4-st rep

Left Mitten
Work same as right mitten, foll chart pats III and IV.

Star (make 4)
With B, cast on 13 sts.

TRIANGLE
Row 1 (WS) K1, p to last st, k1.
Row 2 (RS) K1, ssk, k to last 3 sts, k2tog, k1—11 sts. Rep rows 1 and 2 three times more, then row 1 once—5 sts.
Next row (RS) K1, S2KP, k1.
Next row P3tog. Fasten off last st.

FIRST POINT
With RS of triangle facing and B, skip first 3 sts of cast-on edge, then pick up and k 1 st in each of next 7 sts, leaving last 3 sts unworked—7 sts.
Rep rows 1 and 2 of triangle once, then row 1 once—5 sts. Work last 2 rows of triangle. Fasten off last st.

SECOND POINT
With RS of triangle facing and B, pick up and k 5 sts in center of side edge of triangle. Work last 2 rows of triangle. Fasten off last st.

THIRD POINT
Work same as second point.

Finishing
Block pieces to measurements. Place 2 stars tog with WS facing. Using B, whipstitch edges tog.

I-CORD (MAKE 2)
With dpns and B, cast on 4 sts leaving a long tail for sewing. Work in I-cord as foll: ***Next row (RS)** With 2nd dpn, k4, *do not turn*. Slide sts back to beg of needle to work next row from RS; rep from * for 6"/15cm. Cut yarn leaving a 6"/15cm tail and thread through rem sts. Pull tog tightly, secure end, then sew to first point of a star. Sew opposite end of I-cord to outside edge of mitten at rnd 1 of cuff chart. ■

Stitch Key

☐ Knit

◪ K2tog

◪ Ssk

Ⓜ M1

▨ No stitch

Color Key

▪ Midnight Blue (A)

▪ Blue Hawaii (B)

CHART II

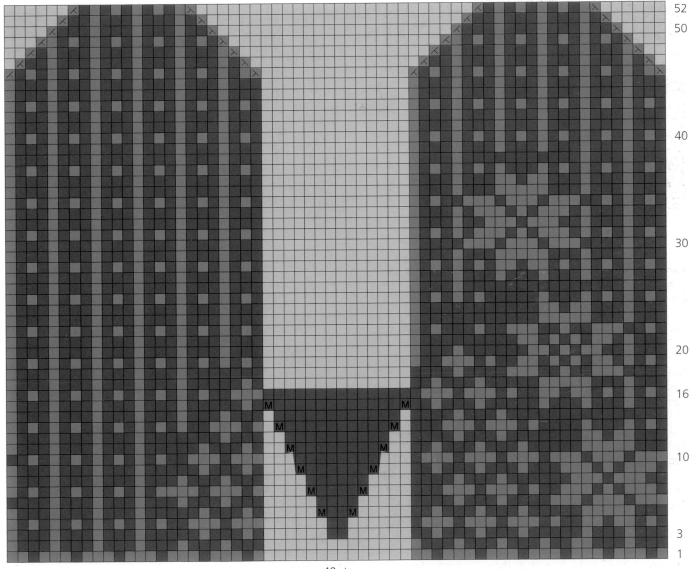

48 sts

 Quick Tip
For a personalized effect, try knitting a different motif—like a
heart, flower or leaf—to dangle from the I-cord tassels.

Star-Motif Mittens

CHART IV

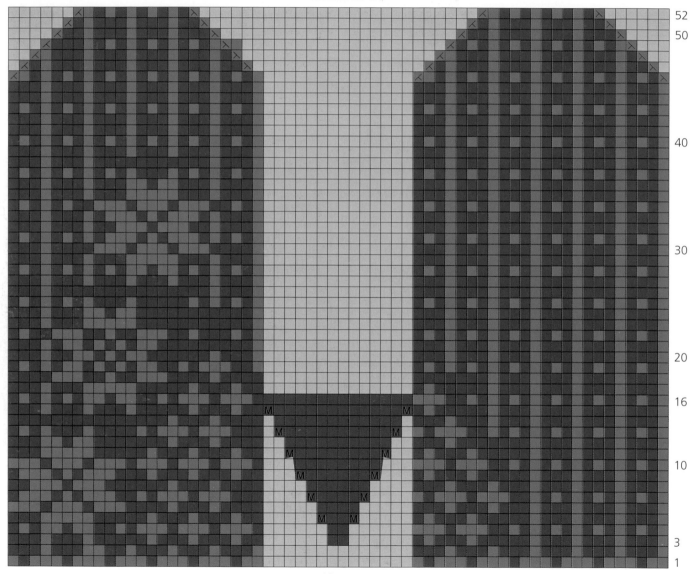

48 sts

I-Cord Squiggle Scarf

Easier than it looks, most of the work is done after the main body has been knit.
Be creative and add as many different colored squiggles as you like.

DESIGNED BY ANGELA JUERGENS

Size
Instructions are written for one size.

Knitted Measurements
Approx 7¼" x 58"/18.5cm x 147.5cm
(excluding fringe)

Materials
■ 4 1¾oz/50g hanks (each approx
164yd/150m) of *Cascade 220 Sport*
(Peruvian highland wool) in #9430
highland green (MC)

■ 1 hank in #8267 forest green (CC)

■ One pair size 6 (4mm) needles *or size to
obtain gauge*

■ Sizes 2 and 6 (2.75 and 4mm) circular
needles, 40"/102cm long

■ Stitch markers

Note
The fringe and waves are added on to
scarf after scarf is knitted.

Scarf
With MC, cast on 47 sts.

BEG CHART PAT
Row 1 (RS) Sl 1 purlwise wyif, pm, work
18-st rep twice, work last 9 sts, pm, k1.
Row 2 Sl 1 purlwise wyif, sl marker,
work first 9 sts, work 18-st rep twice, sl
marker, k1. Keeping 1 st each side in sl
st pat as established, cont to foll chart in
this way to row 28, then rep rows 1–28
seventeen times more. Bind off knitwise.

Gauge
26 sts and 32 rows to 4"/10cm over chart pat using size 6 (4mm) needles
(after fringe and waves have been added). *Take time to check gauge.*

I-Cord Squiggle Scarf

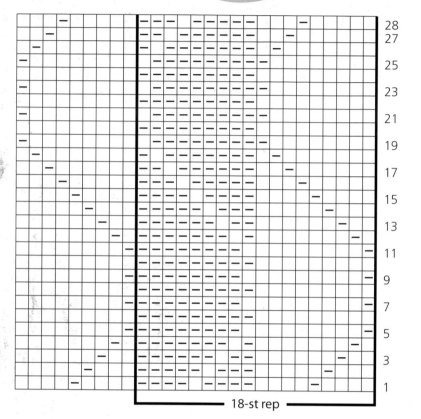

Stitch Key

☐ K on RS, p on WS

⊟ P on RS, k on WS

28 27 25 23 21 19 17 15 13 11 9 7 5 3 1

18-st rep

FRINGE AND WAVES
Pick up purl sts. Position scarf so RS is facing and cast–on edge at your right. Beg with bottom column of wave pat purl sts. Working from right to left along length of scarf, use smaller circular needle and MC to pick up each purl st across to bind off edge.

FRINGE
Row 1 (RS) Using larger circular needle and MC, use the long–tail cast–on method to cast on 30 sts, then knit across all purl sts on smaller circular needle. At the end of row, use the knitted cast–on method to cast on 30 sts.
Row 2 Purl.
Row 3 Knit.
Row 4 Purl. Bind off all sts loosely knitwise. On RS of scarf, rep twice more. On WS of scarf, rep twice using CC. ∎

Flower Chapeau

With a lovely woven slip-stitch pattern and I-cord flower, this charming hat will transition gracefully from winter into spring.

DESIGNED BY SUSAN MINK AND NATALIE DERSE

Size

Instructions are written for one size.

Knitted Measurements

Head circumference 23"/58.5cm
Depth 7½"/19cm

Materials

- 2 1¾oz/50g hanks (each approx 164yd/150m) of *Cascade 220 Sport* (Peruvian highland wool) in #8010 natural (MC)
- 1 hank in #2450 mystic purple (CC)
- Size 4 (3.5mm) circular needle, 16"/40cm long *or size to obtain gauge*
- One set (5) size 4 (3.5mm) double-pointed needles (dpns)
- Cable needle (cn)
- Stitch markers

Short Row Wrap & Turn (w&t)

[on RS row (on WS row)]
1) Wyib (wyif), sl next st pwise.
2) Move yarn between the needles to the front (back).
3) Sl the same st back to LH needle. Turn work. One st is wrapped.
4) When working the wrapped st, insert RH needle under the wrap and work it tog with the corresponding st on needle.

Stitch Glossary

4-st LC Sl 2 sts to cn and hold to front, k2, k2 from cn.
2-st LT With RH needle behind RH needle, skip the first st and k 2nd st tbl, insert RH needle into backs of both sts, k2tog tbl.

Woven Stitch

(multiple of 2 sts)
Rnd 1 Knit.
Rnd 2 *Sl 1 wyif, k1; rep from * around.
Rnd 3 Knit.
Rnd 4 *K1, sl 1 wyif; rep from * around.
Rep rnds 1–4 for woven st.

Hat

BRIM

With circular needle and MC, cast on 134 sts. Join and pm taking care not to twist sts on needle. Work in k1, p1 rib for one rnd.

SHORT ROW SHAPING

Next 2 rows Work in rib over 93 sts, pm, w&t; work in rib over next 3 sts, pm, w&t.

Next 2 rows Work in rib to 2nd marker, drop marker, work next 2 sts working wrap and wrapped st tog, pm (new 2nd marker), w&t; work in rib to first marker, drop marker, work next 2 sts working wrap and wrapped st tog, pm (new first marker), w&t. Rep last 2 rows until there are 71 sts between the first and 2nd markers. Cont to work in the rnd as foll:

Next rnd Work in rib, working rem wrap and wrapped sts tog and dropping extra markers.

Next rnd Work in rib.

Next rnd P. Cont in woven st for 3 ¾"/9.5cm, end with rnd 1 or 3.

Gauge

23 sts and 34 rnds to 4"/10cm over woven st using size 4 (3.5mm) circular needle. *Take time to check gauge.*

Flower Chapeau

CROWN SHAPING
Change to dpns (dividing sts evenly between 4 needles) when there are too few sts on circular needle.
Next (dec) rnd P, dec 6 sts evenly spaced around—128 sts. Cont in cable pat as foll:
Rnds 1–4 *P4, k4; rep from * around.
Rnd 5 *P4, 4-st LC; rep from * around.
Rnd (dec) 6 *P1, p2tog, p1, k4; rep from * around—112 sts.
Rnds 7 and 8 *P3, k4; rep from * around.
Rnd 9 *P3, 4-st LC; rep from * around.
Rnds 10 and 11 *P3, k4; rep from * around.
Rnd (dec) 12 *P1, p2tog, k4; rep from * around—96 sts.
Rnd 13 *P2, 4-st LC; rep from * around.
Rnds 14 and 15 *P2, k4; rep from * around.
Rnd (dec) 16 *P2, sl 2 sts to cn, k2tog, k2tog from cn; rep from * around—64 sts.
Rnds 17 and 18 *P2, k2; rep from * around.
Rnd (dec) 19 *p2tog, 2-st LT; rep from * around—48 sts.
Rnd 20 *P1, k2; rep from * around.
Rnd (dec) 21 *P1, k2tog; rep from * around—32 sts.
Rnd (dec) 22 [K2tog] 16 times—16 sts.
Rnd (dec) 23 [K2tog] 8 times—8 sts.
Rnd (dec) 24 [K2tog] 4 times—4 sts.
Cut yarn leaving an 8"/20.5cm tail and thread through rem sts. Pull tog tightly and secure end.

Flower
FIRST ROW OF PETALS
With dpns and CC, cast on 3 sts leaving a long tail for sewing. Work in I-cord as

foll: ***Next row (RS)** With 2nd dpn, k3, do not turn. Slide sts back to beg of needle to work next row from RS; rep from * until I-cord measures 15"/38cm from beg. Cut yarn, leaving a long tail for sewing. Thread tail in tapestry needle, then thread through rem sts. Working on a soft surface (such as a throw pillow), form and pin I-cord into five 1½"/4cm-long petal loops. Tack bottom edges of loops in center to secure them in place.

SECOND ROW OF PETALS
Make a 15"/38cm I-cord. Form and pin I-cord into six 1¼"/3cm-long petal loops. Tack bottom edges of loops in center to secure them in place. Sew center of second row of petals to center of first row of petals. Fold ribbed brim of hat over to RS. Sew center of flower to widest part of brim, going through all layers to secure both flower and brim in place as shown. ■

Wave-Cuff Mittens

In this clever twist on a popular lace pattern, lacy cuffs are knit separately from the mittens and attached later. Dive into your button stash for the perfect finishing touch.

DESIGNED BY EDNA HART

Size
Instructions are written for one size.

Knitted Measurements
Hand circumference 7"/18cm
Length of cuff approx 3"/7.5cm

Materials
- 1 1¾oz/50g hank (each approx 164yd/150m) of *Cascade 220 Sport* (Peruvian highland wool) each in #4010 straw (MC) and #9448 olive heather (CC)
- One pair size 6 (4mm) needles *or size to obtain gauge*
- One set (5) size 5 (3.75mm) double-pointed needles (dpns) *or size to obtain gauge*
- Size E/4 (3.5mm) crochet hook
- Stitch markers
- Two ⅝"/16mm buttons

Note
Cuffs and mittens are made separately, then sewn tog.

Stitch Glossary
M1R (make 1 right) Insert left needle from back to front into the horizontal strand between the last st worked and the next st on left needle. K this strand through the front lp to twist the st.
M1L (make 1 left) Insert left needle from front to back into the horizontal strand between the last st worked and the next st on left needle. K this strand tbl to twist the st.

Cuff (make 2)
With straight needles and MC, cast on 60 sts. K next 3 rows. Change to CC.

BEG CHART PAT
Row 1 (RS) Work 60 sts of chart. Cont to foll chart in this way to row 20—46 sts. Change to MC. K next row.
Bind off kwise.

Mitten (make 2)
With dpns and MC, cast on 45 sts. Divide sts over 4 needles. Join, taking care not to twist sts on needles, pm for beg of rnds. Cont in St st (k every rnd) for 4 rnds.

THUMB GUSSET
Inc rnd 1 K22, pm, M1L, k1, M1R, pm, k22—47 sts.
Knit next rnd.
Inc rnd 2 K to marker, sl marker, M1L, k to next marker, M1R, sl marker, k to end of rnd—49 sts.
Knit next 2 rnds.
Rep last 3 rnds 6 times more—61 sts (17 sts between thumb gusset markers).
Next rnd K to marker, drop marker, place next 17 sts on scrap yarn for thumb, drop marker, cast on 1 st, k to end of rnd—45 sts.

Gauges
25 sts to 4"/10cm and 20 rows to 3"/7.5cm over chart pat using size 6 (4mm) needles.
26 sts and 36 rnds to 4"/10cm over St st using size 5 (3.75mm) dpns. *Take time to check gauges.*

Wave-Cuff Mittens

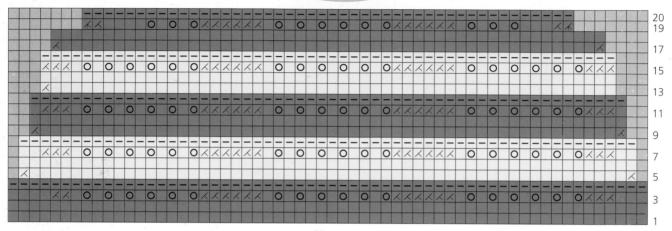

60 sts

HAND
Work even in St st until piece measures 5"/12.5cm from beg, dec 1 st at end of last rnd—44 sts.

TOP SHAPING
Dec rnd 1 [K9, k2tog] 4 times—40 sts. K next rnd.
Dec rnd 2 [K8, k2tog] 4 times—36 sts. K next rnd.
Dec rnd 3 [K7, k2tog] 4 times—32 sts. K next rnd.
Dec rnd 4 [K6, k2tog] 4 times—28 sts. K next rnd.
Dec rnd 5 [K5, k2tog] 4 times—24 sts.
Dec rnd 6 [K4, k2tog] 4 times—20 sts.
Dec rnd 7 [K3, k2tog] 4 times—16 sts.
Dec rnd 8 [K2, k2tog] 4 times—12 sts.
Dec rnd 9 [K1, k2tog] 4 times—8 sts.
Dec rnd 10 [K2tog] 4 times—4 sts.
Cut yarn leaving a 6"/15cm tail and thread through rem sts. Pull tog tightly and secure end.

THUMB
Place 17 thumb gusset sts over 2 needles.

Next rnd Join yarn and k across sts, then pick up and k 1 st over cast-on of opening—18 sts. Divide sts evenly over 3 needles. Join and pm for beg of rnds. Cont in St st for 1½"/4cm.

TOP SHAPING
Dec rnd 1 [K1, k2tog] 6 times—12 sts. K next rnd.
Dec rnd 2 [K1, k2tog] 4 times—8 sts. K next rnd.
Dec rnd 3 [K2tog] 4 times—4 sts.
Cut yarn leaving a 6"/15cm tail and thread through rem sts. Pull tog tightly and secure end.

Finishing
For right mitten, sew top edge of cuff to bottom edge of mitten so cuff opening is centered on the palm side (thumb will be at right). For left mitten, sew top edge of cuff to bottom edge of mitten so cuff opening is centered on the palm side (thumb will be at left).

EDGING
With RS facing and crochet hook, join

Stitch Key
☐ K on RS, p on WS
− K on WS
Ⓞ Yarn over
⟋ K2tog
⟋ K3tog
▨ No stitch

Color Key
☐ Straw (MC)
▨ Olive Heather (CC)

MC with a sl st at base of cuff opening. Ch 1, sc evenly around edge, working 3 sc in each corner, join rnd with a sl st in first sc. Fasten off.

BUTTON LOOP (MAKE 2)
With crochet hook and MC, ch 11 leaving a long tail for sewing. Fasten off leaving a long tail for sewing. For right mitten, have palm side facing, then sew button lp to left bottom corner of cuff. For left mitten, have palm side facing, then sew button lp to right bottom corner of cuff. Sew buttons onto corners opposite button lps. ■

Diamond-Leaf Lace Scarf

Bedeck your neck in elegance with this feminine lace scarf. It is knit in two pieces in an allover diamond-leaf lace pattern and grafted together at the center.

DESIGNED BY MARI TOBITA

Size
Instructions are written for one size.

Knitted Measurements
Width (widest part) 9"/23cm
Length 62"/157.5cm

Materials
- 4 1¾ oz/50g hanks (each approx 164yd/150m) of *Cascade 220 Sport* (Peruvian highland wool) in #2450 mystic purple
- One pair size 5 (3.75 mm) and size 6 (4mm) needles or size to obtain gauge
- Stitch holder

Stitch Glossary
M1R Insert LH needle from back to front under the strand between last st worked and the next st on the LH needle. Knit into the front loop to twist the st.
M1L Insert the LH needle from front to back under the strand between last st worked and the next st on the LH needle. Knit into the back loop to twist the st.
S2KP (center double decrease) Sl 2 sts tog as if to knit, k1, pass 2 sl sts over k1.

Note
Scarf is worked in 2 pieces and grafted at the center.

Scarf (make 2)
With smaller needles, cast on 59 sts using knitted cast-on.
Rows 1, 3 and 4 K1, p to last st, k1.
Row 2 K1, p1, *yo, p2tog; rep from * to last st, k1.
Change to larger needles.

BEG CHART I
Row 1 K1, work row 1 to rep line, work 14-st rep once more, work to end of chart row, k1.
Cont to work chart in this manner, knitting first and last st of every row, until rows 1–24 have been worked 3 times, rep rows 1–10 once more.
Next (dec) row (RS) K1, ssk, [k11, S2KP] 3 times, k11, k2tog, k1—51 sts.
Next row K1, p to last st, k1.

BEG CHART II
Next row (RS) K1, work row 11 of chart II to rep line, work 12-st rep once more, work to end of chart row, k1.
Next row K1, work row 12 of chart II to rep line, work 12-st rep once more, work to end of chart row, k1.
Cont to work chart II in this manner, knitting first and last st of every row, until row 20 is complete. Work rows 1–20 three times, then rep rows 1–8 once more.
Next (dec) row (RS) K1, ssk, [k9, S2KP] 3 times, k9, k2tog, k1—43 sts.
Next row K1, p to last st, k1.

BEG CHART III
Next row (RS) K1, work row 9 of chart 3 to rep line, work 10-st rep once more, work to end of chart row, k1.
Cont to work chart III in this manner, knitting first and last st of every row, until row 16 is complete. Work rows 1–16 five times, then rep rows 1–8 once more. Place sts on st holder.

Finishing
Block scarf.
Join halves tog using Kitchener st. ■

Gauges
24 sts and 31 rows to 4"/10cm over St st using larger needles.
27 sts and 35 rows to 4"/10cm over chart 1 pat using larger needles.
27 sts and 34 rows to 4"/10cm over chart 2 pat using larger needles.
28 sts and 34 rows to 4"/10cm over chart 3 pat using larger needles. *Take time to check gauges.*

Diamond-Leaf Lace Scarf

CHART I

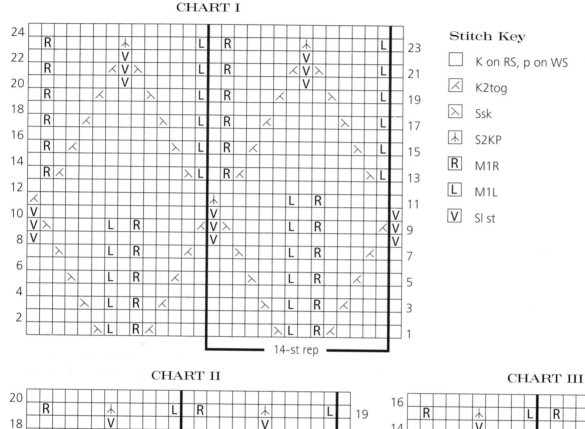

14-st rep

Stitch Key

☐	K on RS, p on WS
⟋	K2tog
⟍	Ssk
⅄	S2KP
R	M1R
L	M1L
V	Sl st

CHART II

12-st rep

CHART III

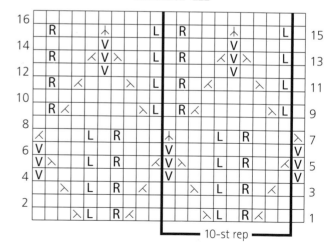

10-st rep

Cabled Beanie

This simple beanie is dressed up with cables and bobbles that add texture and whimsical detail.

DESIGNED BY NICHOLE REESE

Size
Instructions are written for one size.

Knitted Measurements
Head circumference 20"/51cm
Depth 7¾"/19.5cm

Materials
■ 2 1¾oz/50g hanks (each approx 164yd/150m) of *Cascade 220 Sport* (Peruvian highland wool) in #8894 Christmas green
■ Size 5 (3.75mm) circular needle, 16"/40cm long *or size to obtain gauge*
■ One set (5) size 5 (3.75mm) double-pointed needles (dpns)
■ Cable needle (cn)
■ Stitch markers

Stitch Glossary
4–st RC Sl 2 sts to cn and hold to *back,* k2, k2 from cn.
4–st LC Sl 2 sts to cn and hold to *front,* k2, k2 from cn.
Make bobble (MB) [Yo, k1] 3 times in next st, turn; [sl1 wyif, p5, turn; sl1 wyib, k5, turn] twice; [p2tog] 3 times, turn; SK2P.

Beanie
With circular needle, cast on 144 sts. Join and pm, taking care not to twist sts on needle.

Set-up rnd *P4, k8; rep from * around. Rep this rnd once more.

BEG CHART PAT
Rnd 1 Work 48–st rep 3 times. Cont to foll chart in this way to rnd 6, then rep rnds 1–6 twice more.
Rnd 7 Work 48–st rep 3 times. Cont to foll chart in this way to rnd 18, then rep rnds 7–17 once more.
Rnd 18 Work 48–st rep 3 times, ending 4 sts before end of rnd, pm for new beg of rnd; drop old marker when you come to it.

CROWN SHAPING
Change to dpns (dividing sts evenly between 4 needles) when there are too few sts on circular needle.
Rnd 19 Work 48–st rep 3 times. Cont to foll chart in this way to rnd 34—12 sts.
Next rnd [Ssk, k1] 4 times—8 sts.
Cut yarn leaving an 8"/20.5cm tail and thread through rem sts. Pull tog tightly and secure end. ■

Gauge
26 sts and 36 rnds to 4"/10cm over St st using size 5 (3.75mm) circular needle. *Take time to check gauge.*

Cabled Beanie

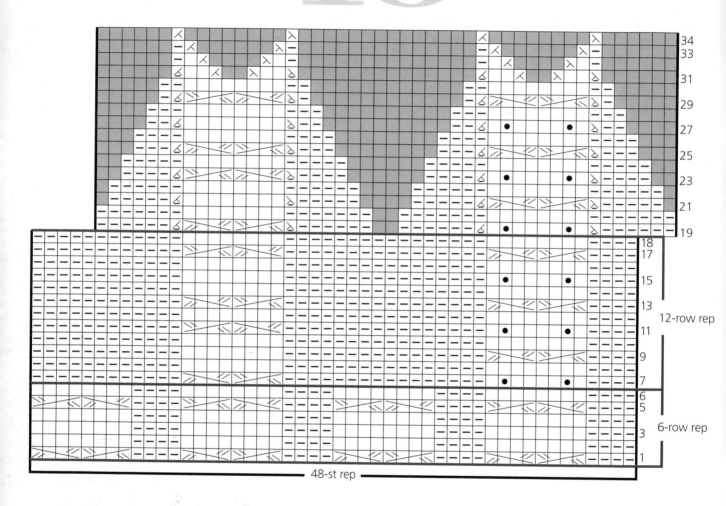

34 · 33 · 31 · 29 · 27 · 25 · 23 · 21 · 19

18 · 17 · 15 · 13 · 11 · 9 · 7 — 12-row rep

6 · 5 · 3 · 1 — 6-row rep

48-st rep

Stitch Key

☐	Knit		◹	P2tog tbl
—	Purl		⤬	4-st RC
⟋	K2tog		⤬	4-st LC
⟍	Ssk		●	MB (Make Bobble)
◸	P2tog		▩	No stitch

Nordic Mittens

These Norwegian-style mittens have cuffs of corrugated rib, a picot edging and a classic winter color combination. They're perfect to wear while sledding or throwing snowballs.

DESIGNED BY HEIDI TODD KOZAR

Size
Instructions are written for one size.

Knitted Measurements
Hand circumference 7½"/19cm
Length of cuff Approx 2½"/6.5cm

Materials
■ 1 1¾oz/50g hank (each approx 164yd/150m) of *Cascade 220 Sport* (Peruvian highland wool) each in #9404 ruby (MC), #8010 natural (A) and #8400 charcoal grey (B)
■ One set (5) each sizes 3 and 5 (3.25 and 3.75mm) double-pointed needles (dpns) *or size to obtain gauge*
■ Stitch marker

Notes
1) To work in the rnd, always read charts from right to left.
2) Centers of snowflakes are worked in duplicate stitch after knitting is completed.

Mitten (make 2)
CUFF
With smaller dpns and MC, cast on 44 sts. Divide sts over 4 needles (11 sts on each). Join, taking care not to twist sts on needles, pm for beg of rnds. Cont in St st (knit every rnd) for 9 rnds. Change to B. Knit next 2 rnds.
Next (picot) rnd *Yo, k2tog; rep from * around.
Next (inc) rnd Knit, inc 4 sts evenly spaced around—48 sts. Knit next rnd. Change to larger dpns.

BEG CHART PAT I
Beg chart on rnd 1 and work even through rnd 19.

THUMB GUSSET
Rnd 20 Work first 24 sts of chart, with MC, M1, with A, k1, with MC, M1, work to end of rnd—50 sts. Cont to foll chart in this way through rnd 40, working inc as shown—62 sts.
Rnd 41 Work first 24 sts of chart, place 15 thumb sts on scrap yarn, with MC, cast on 1 st over thumb opening, work to end of rnd—48 sts. Cont to work to top of chart, dec top of mitten as shown—8 sts. Cut MC leaving a 6"/15cm tail and thread through rem sts. Pull tog tightly and secure end. Cut A and weave in end.

THUMB
Place 15 sts on scrap yarn on 2 dpns (7 sts on first needle and 8 sts on 2nd needle). With 3rd needle and MC, pick up and k 1 st in cast-on st of thumb opening, then 2 sts along side edge of thumb opening, k 7 sts on first needle, 8 sts on 2nd needle, then with 4th needle, pick up and k 2 sts along side edge of thumb opening, pm for beg of rnds—20 sts. Divide sts evenly over 4 needles (5 sts on each).

BEG CHART II
Beg chart on rnd 1 and work to top of chart, working dec as shown—6 sts. Cut MC leaving a 6"/15cm tail and thread through rem sts. Pull tog tightly and secure end. Cut A and weave in end.

Finishing
Turn bottom edges to WS along picot rnd and hem in place. Use MC tail to sew gap between thumb and hand closed.

DUPLICATE STITCH EMBROIDERY
Referring to chart pats, work one duplicate stitch in center of each snowflake using B. Block pieces to measurements. ■

Gauge
26 sts and 28 rnds to 4"/10cm over chart pats using larger dpns. *Take time to check gauge.*

Nordic Mittens

CHART II

20 sts

Color Key

■ Ruby (MC)

□ Natural (A)

▨ Charcoal Grey (B)

Stitch Key

□ Knit

− Purl

Ⓜ M1

╱ K2tog

╲ Ssk

⋁ Duplicate st using B

▨ No stitch

DUPLICATE STITCH
Duplicate stitch covers a knit stitch. Bring the needle up below the stitch to be worked. Insert the needle under both loops one row above and pull it through. Insert it back into the stitch below and through the center of the next stitch in one motion, as shown.

Quick Tip
Duplicate stitching is the perfect way to add different colored stitches without carrying the yarn across an entire round. It's also a clever way to fix any mistakes without having to rip out your knitting.

CHART I

71
70

60

50

40

30

20

10

1

48 sts

Ruffle-Edge Lace Scarf

You'll go from ruffles to riches in this pretty scarf. With an easy-to-memorize lace pattern between ruffled edgings, this scarf adds a feminine touch to any outfit.

DESIGNED BY LINDA MEDINA

Size

Instructions are written for one size.

Knitted Measurements

Approx 6½ " x 56"/16.5cm x 142cm

Materials

■ 4 1¾oz/50g hanks (each approx 164yd/150m) of *Cascade 220 Sport* (Peruvian highland wool) in #7805 flamingo pink

■ One pair size 6 (4mm) needles *or size to obtain gauge*

■ Stitch markers

Stitch Glossary

M1L Insert LH needle (from front to back) under horizontal strand between next 2 sts, then p1 through back lp.

M1R Insert LH needle (front back to front) under horizontal strand between next 2 sts, then p1 through front lp.

Lace Pattern

(multiple of 3 sts plus 2)
Row 1 (RS) P2, *yo, k1, yo, p2; rep from * to end.
Row 2 K2, *p3, k2; rep from * to end.
Row 3 P2, *k3, p2; rep from * to end.
Row 4 K2, *p3tog, k2; rep from * to end.
Rep rows 1–4 for lace pat.

Scarf

Cast on 111 sts.

BOTTOM RUFFLE
Row 1 (RS) P3, *k9, p3; rep from * to end.
Row 2 K3, *p9, k3; rep from * to end.
Row 3 P3, *ssk, k5, k2tog, p3; rep from * to end.
Row 4 K3, *p7, k3; rep from * to end.
Row 5 P3, *ssk, k3, k2tog, p3; rep from * to end.
Row 6 K3, *p5, k3; rep from * to end.
Row 7 P3, *ssk, k1, k2tog, p3; rep from * to end.
Row 8 K3, *p3, k3; rep from * to end.
Row 9 P3, *SK2P, p3; rep from * to end—39 sts.
Row 10 K3, *p1, k3; rep from * to end.
Cont in lace pat as foll:
Next row (RS) K2, pm, work row 1 of lace pat to last 2 sts, pm, k2.

Next row K2, sl marker, work row 2 of lace pat to next marker, sl marker, k2. Keeping 2 sts each side in garter st (knit every row), cont to work rem sts in lace pat until piece measures approx 53½"/138.5cm from beg, end with row 4 of lace pat.

TOP RUFFLE
Row 1 (RS) P3, *k1, p3; rep from * to end.
Row 2 K3, *M1L, p1, M1R, k3; rep from * to end.
Row 3 P3, *k3, p3; rept from * to end.
Row 4 K3, *M1L, p3, M1R, k3; rep from * to end.
Row 5 P3, *k5, p3; rep from * to end.
Row 6 K3, *M1L, p5, M1R, k3; rep from * to end.
Row 7 P3, *k7, p3; rep from * to end.
Row 8 K3, *M1L, p7, M1R, k3; rep from * to end—111 sts.
Row 9 P3, *k9, p3; rep from * to end.
Row 10 K3, *p9, k3; rep from * to end.
Bind off in pat st. *Do not block.* ■

Gauge

24 sts and 30 rows to 4"/10cm over lace pat using size 6 (4mm) needles. *Take time to check gauge.*

Birdcage Beanie

You'll be cuckoo for this fun-to-knit hat. The simple intarsia cage and bird are accented with an added-on beak, eye and feet. Change the colors to match your favorite budgie.

DESIGNED BY AMY BAHRT

Size
Instructions are written for one size.

Knitted Measurements
Head circumference 19"/48cm
Depth 8"/20.5cm

Materials
■ 1 1¾oz/50g hank (each approx 164yd/150m) of *Cascade 220 Sport* (Peruvian highland wool) each in #8906 blue topaz (MC), #7827 goldenrod (A), #2453 pumpkin spice (B) and #8910 citron (C)
■ One pair each sizes 4 and 5 (3.5 and 3.75mm) needles *or size to obtain gauge*
■ Size G/6 (4mm) crochet hook
■ Bobbins (optional)
■ One ⅜"/10mm 4-hole shirt button in white
■ Dark brown sewing thread

Notes
1) Use a separate bobbin (or strand) of A for each birdcage rib.
2) Use 1 strand of MC for all rows below and above bird. When working rows 3–25 of chart pat, use a separate strand of MC for each side of bird.
3) When changing colors, pick up new color from under dropped color to prevent holes.

Hat
With smaller needles and A, cast on 114 sts. Work in St st (knit on RS, purl on WS) for 4 rows, end with a WS row.
Cont in k1, p1 rib for 6 rows, end with a WS row. Change to larger needles. Cont in St st as foll:

BIRDCAGE PAT
Row 1 (RS) [K2 with A, k12 with MC] 8 times, k2 with A.
Row 2 [P2 with A, p12 with MC] 8 times, p2 with A. Rep last 2 rows 3 times more.

BEG CHART PAT
Row 1 (RS) With A, knit.
Row 2 With A, purl.
Row 3 (RS) [K2 with A, k12 with MC] 3 times, work 30 sts of chart (starting on row 3), [k12 with MC, K2 with A] 3 times. Cont to foll chart in this way to

row 28, end with a WS row. Change to 1 strand A. Knit 1 row, purl 1 row.

CROWN SHAPING
Dec row 1 (RS) [K2 with A, k10 with MC, k2tog with MC] 8 times, k2 with A— 106. Purl next row in color pat as established.
Dec row 2 [K2 with A, k9 with MC, k2tog with MC] 8 times, k2 with A—98. Purl next row in color pat as established.
Dec row 3 [K2 with A, k8 with MC, k2tog with MC] 8 times, k2 with A—90. Purl next row in color pat as established.
Dec row 4 [K2 with A, k7 with MC, k2tog with MC] 8 times, k2 with A—82. Purl next row in color pat as established. Change to A only.
Dec row 5 [K8, k2tog] 8 times, k2—74 sts. Purl next row.
Dec row 6 [K7, k2tog] 8 times, k2—66 sts. Purl next row.
Dec row 7 [K6, k2tog] 8 times, k2—58 sts. Purl next row.
Dec row 8 [K5, k2tog] 8 times, k2—50 sts. Purl next row.
Dec row 9 [K4, k2tog] 8 times, k2—42 sts. Purl next row.
Dec row 10 [K3, k2tog] 8 times, k2—34 sts. Purl next row.

Gauge
24 sts and 32 rows to 4"/10cm over St st using larger needles. *Take time to check gauge.*

13 Birdcage Beanie

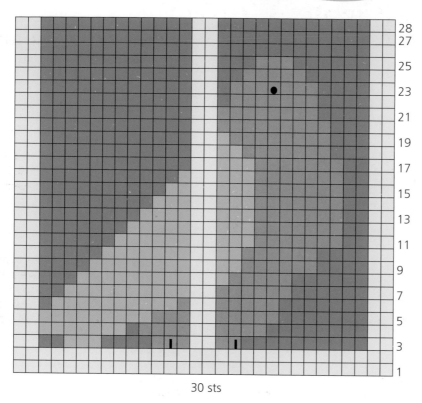

28
27
25
23
21
19
17
15
13
11
9
7
5
3
1

30 sts

Stitch Key

■ Blue Topaz (MC)
□ Goldenrod (A)
■ Pumpkin Spice (B)
■ Citron (C)

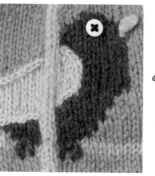

WHIPSTITCH

Symbol Key

● Eye placement

| Attach feet

Dec row 11 [K2, k2tog] 8 times, k2—26 sts. Purl next row.

Dec row 12 [K2tog] 13 times—13 sts. Cut yarn leaving a 20"/51cm tail and thread through rem sts. Pull tog tightly, secure end, then sew back seam.

Finishing

BEAK
With crochet hook and C, ch 9. Fasten off, leaving a long tail for sewing. Fold chain in half so bottom lps are tog, then whipstitch lps tog to secure. Referring to photo for position, sew on beak.

EYE
Using thread doubled in needle, sew on button, stitching through holes forming an X, as shown in photo.

FEET (MAKE 2) AND WING
With crochet hook and B, ch 9 leaving a long tail. Fasten off, leaving a long tail. Using a separate strand of B, attach the center of the chain with vertical straight stitches where indicated on chart; fasten off securely on WS. To form claws, thread one tail into needle, then insert needle below horizontal A stripe (perch); fasten off securely on WS. Rep using rem tail. Outline wing in chain stitch using C. ■

Colorblock Cap

Short rows have you flustered? Master the technique with this multicolored beanie. Worked section-by-section with the ribbed band added last, this hat fits together like a jigsaw puzzle.

DESIGNED BY CAROL J. SULCOSKI

Size
Instructions are written for one size.

Knitted Measurements
Head circumference 19"/48cm
Depth 7½"/19cm

Materials
■ 2 1¾oz/50g hanks (each approx 164yd/150m) of *Cascade 220 Sport* (Peruvian highland wool) in #8400 charcoal grey (MC)

■ 1 hank each in #9454 rainier heather (A), #4010 straw (B), #9459 yakima heather (C), #2452 turtle (D) and #9448 olive heather (E)

■ Contrasting worsted-weight cotton (waste yarn)

■ One pair size 8 (5mm) needles *or size to obtain gauge*

■ Size 8 (5mm) circular needle, 16"/40cm long

■ Size H/8 (5mm) crochet hook (for chain-st provisional cast-on)

■ Stitch marker

Notes
1) Use a double strand of yarn throughout.
2) Hat is worked vertically using short rows to create crown shaping.
3) Ribbed band is added after hat is completed.

Short Row Wrap & Turn (w&t; on RS rows)
1) Wyib, sl next st purlwise.
2) Move yarn between the needles to the front.

3) Sl the same st back to LH needle. Turn work. One st is wrapped.
4) When working the wrapped st, insert RH needle under the wrap and knit it tog with the corresponding st on needle.

Hat
With crochet hook and waste yarn, ch 33 for chain-st provisional cast-on.
Cut yarn and draw end though lp on hook. Turn ch so bottom lps are at top and cut end is at left. With straight needles, and MC and A held tog, beg 2 lps from right end, pick up and k 1 st in each of next 28 lps——28 sts.
Purl next row.

FIRST SECTION
Row 1 K26, w&t.
Row 2 Purl.
Row 3 K25, w&t.
Row 4 Purl.
Row 5 K24, w&t.
Row 6 Purl.
Row 7 K23, w&t.
Row 8 Purl.
Row 9 K22, w&t.
Row 10 Purl.
Row 11 K21, w&t.
Row 12 Purl.

Gauge
16 sts and 24 rows to 4"/10cm over St st using double strand of yarn and size 8 (5mm) needles.
Take time to check gauge.

45

Colorblock Cap

Row 13 K20, w&t.
Row 14 Purl.
Row 15 K19, w&t.
Row 16 Purl.
Row 17 K18, w&t.
Row 18 Purl.
Row 19 K17, w&t.
Row 20 Purl. Cut A and join B. With MC and B held tog, cont as foll:
Next row (RS) Knit to end, picking up wraps.
Next row Purl.

SECOND SECTION
With MC and B held tog, rep rows 1–20 same as first section. Cut B and join C. With MC and C held tog, work last 2 rows.

THIRD SECTION
With MC and C held tog, rep rows 1–20 same as first section. Cut C and join D. With MC and D held tog, work last 2 rows.

FOURTH SECTION
With MC and D held tog, rep rows 1–20 same as first section. Cut D and join E. With MC and E held tog, work last 2 rows.

FIFTH SECTION
With MC and E held tog, rep rows 1–20 same as first section.
Next row (RS) Knit to end, picking up wraps. Cut yarns leaving 18"/45.5cm tails. With RS facing, release cut end from lp of waste yarn ch. Pulling out 1 ch at a time, place 28 live sts onto spare straight needle ready for a RS row. Graft sts from first section and last section tog using Kitchener st. Thread 1 strand of MC into tapestry needle. Sew running sts around top edge. Pull tog tightly to close opening and secure end.

RIBBED BAND
With RS facing, circular needle and 2 strands of MC held tog, beg at seam and pick up and k 80 sts evenly spaced around bottom edge. Join and pm for beg of rnds. Purl next 2 rnds. Cont in k3, p1 rib for 6 rnds. Bind off loosely in rib. ■

Quick Tip
Online tutorials are a great way to get some extra help with tricky techniques, like short-row-shaping.

Cables and Leaves Fingerless Mitts

These nature-inspired beauties start with a simple ribbed cuff and feature cables and lace worked only on the front sides. Wear them while hiking in the forest or visiting the botanical garden in the city.

DESIGNED BY JACQUELINE VAN DILLEN

Size
Instructions are written for one size.

Knitted Measurements
Length 12"/30.5cm

Materials
- 2 1¾ oz/50g hanks (each approx 164yd/150m) of *Cascade 220 Sport* (Peruvian highland wool) in #9451 lake chelan heather
- One pair size 3 (3.25mm) needles, or size to obtain gauge
- One set (4) size 3 (3.25mm) double-pointed needles (dpns) or size to obtain gauge
- Waste yarn or stitch holder
- Cable needle (cn)

Stitch Glossary
SK2P Sl 1, k2tog, pass slipped st over the k2tog for a left slanting double dec.
3-st RC Sl 1 to cn and hold to back, k2, k1 from cn.
3-st LC Sl 1 to cn and hold to front, k2, k1 from cn.
6-st RC Sl 3 sts to cn and hold to back, k3, k3 from cn.
6-st LC Sl 3 sts to cn and hold to front, k3, k3 from cn.

K1, P1 Ribbing
(over an even number of sts)
Row 1 *K1, p1; rep from * to end.
Row 2 K the knit sts and p the purl sts.
Rep row 2 for k1, p1 rib.

Right Mitt
With straight needles, cast on 54 sts. Work in k1, p1 ribbing for 1¾"/4.5 cm.

BEG CHARTS
Next row (RS) K1, work row 1 of chart I over 10 sts, work row 1 of chart II over 9 sts, work row 1 of chart III over 10 sts, k24.
Next row (WS) K1, p23, work row 2 of chart III over 10 sts, work row 2 of chart II over 9 sts, work row 2 of chart I over 10 sts, k1.
Cont to work charts in this manner until row 20 is complete.
Rep rows 1–20 twice more and then 1–18 once.

THUMB PLACEMENT
Next row (RS) K1, work chart pats as established over 29 sts, sl next 7 sts to scrap yarn or holder for thumb, cast on 7 sts, work to end of row.
Next row K the knit sts and p the purl sts. Work in k1, p1 ribbing for 1.25"/3cm. Bind off.

THUMB
Place sts from holder on dpns, rejoin yarn and pick up and k 7 sts along cast-on edge of thumb opening. Divide sts over 3 needles. Knit 1 rnd, increasing 4 sts evenly around—18 sts. Work in k1, p1 rib for 1.25"/3cm. Bind off.

Gauge
24 sts and 36 rows to 4"/10cm over St st using size 3 (3.25mm) needles. *Take time to check gauge.*

Cables and Leaves Fingerless Mitts

CHART I

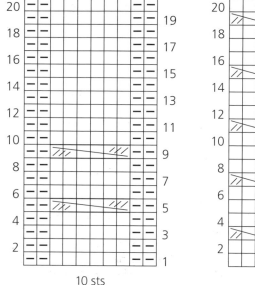

10 sts

CHART II

9-17-9 sts

CHART III

10 sts

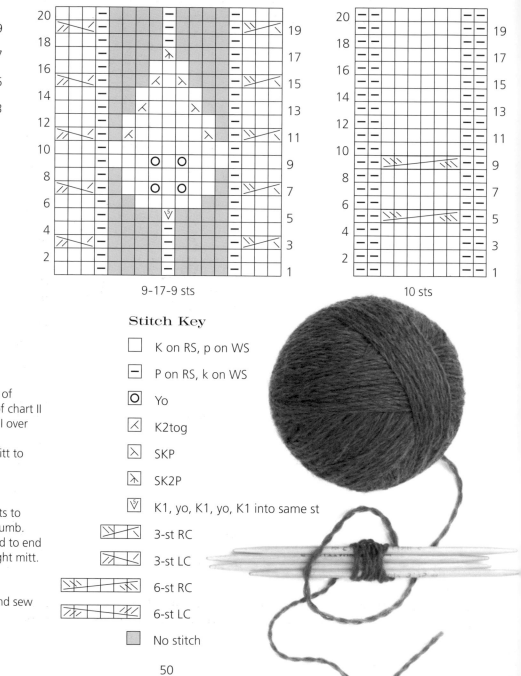

Left Mitt
Work same as for right mitt to beg charts.

BEG CHARTS
Next row (RS) K24, work row 1 of chart I over 10 sts, work row 1 of chart II over 9 sts, work row 1 of chart III over 10 sts, k1.
Cont in same manner as right mitt to thumb placement.

THUMB PLACEMENT
Next row (RS) K17, slip next 7 sts to scrap yarn or stitch holder for thumb. Cast on 7 sts. Cont as established to end of row. Complete same as for right mitt.

Finishing
Block pieces to measurements and sew side seams. ∎

Stitch Key

☐	K on RS, p on WS
—	P on RS, k on WS
O	Yo
⟋	K2tog
⟍	SKP
⅄	SK2P
⅀	K1, yo, k1, yo, k1 into same st
	3-st RC
	3-st LC
	6-st RC
	6-st LC
▨	No stitch

16

Basketweave Pocket Scarf

As utilitarian as it is fun to wear, this basketweave scarf has a pocket on either end to hold all of your treasures. The bobbled argyle pattern adds a classic touch.

DESIGNED BY KATHY NORTH

Size
Instructions are written for one size.

Knitted Measurements
Width 7"/18cm
Length 64"/162.5cm

Materials
■ 4 1¾ oz/50g hanks (each approx 164yd/150m) of *Cascade 220 Sport* (Peruvian highland wool) in #8401 silver grey

■ One pair size 6 (4mm) needles, *or size to obtain gauge*

Notes
1) Scarf body is worked in one piece in three alternating sections: seed stitch, basketweave stitch, seed stitch.
2) Pocket panels are worked separately following chart, then sewn to scarf ends with overcast stitch.

Stitch Glossary
SEED STITCH
(multiple of 2 sts + 1)
Row 1 (RS) *K1, p1; rep from * to last st, k1.
Row 2 & all following rows Rep row 1 (i.e., k the purl sts and p the knit sts as they face you).

BASKETWEAVE STITCH
(multiple of 8 sts + 8)
Row 1 (RS) K2, *K4, p4; rep from * to last 6 sts, k4, k2.
Row 2 (WS) K2, *P4, k4; rep from * to last 6 sts, p4, k2.
Rows 3–4 Rep rows 1–2.

Row 5 K2, *P4, k4; rep from * to last 6 sts, p4, k2.
Row 6 K2, *K4, p4; rep from * to last 6 sts, k4, k2.
Rows 7–8 Rep rows 5–6.
Rep rows 1–8 for basketweave st.

BOBBLE
Row 1 (RS) Kf&b twice in same st, turn work.
Row 2 (WS) P4, turn work.
Row 3 Sl 2, k2tog, p2sso.
On next row, push bobble to front of work.

Scarf
POCKET PANEL (MAKE 2)
Cast on 39 sts.
Work in seed st for 6 rows.

CHART PREPARATION ROWS
Next row (RS) Work in seed st for 5 sts, k to last 5 sts, work in seed st for 5 sts.
Next row (WS) Work in seed st for 5 sts, p to last 5 sts, work in seed st for 5 sts.

BEGIN CHART
Row 1 Work in seed st for 5 sts, work row 1 of chart over 29 sts, seed st 5 sts.
Rows 2–54 Keeping 5 sts at each edge in seed st, follow chart through completion of row 54.

Gauges
22 sts and 30 rows to 4"/10cm over St st using size 6 (4 mm) needles. 23 sts and 34 rows to 4"/10cm over basketweave st using size 6 (4 mm) needles. *Take time to check gauges.*

Basketweave Pocket Scarf

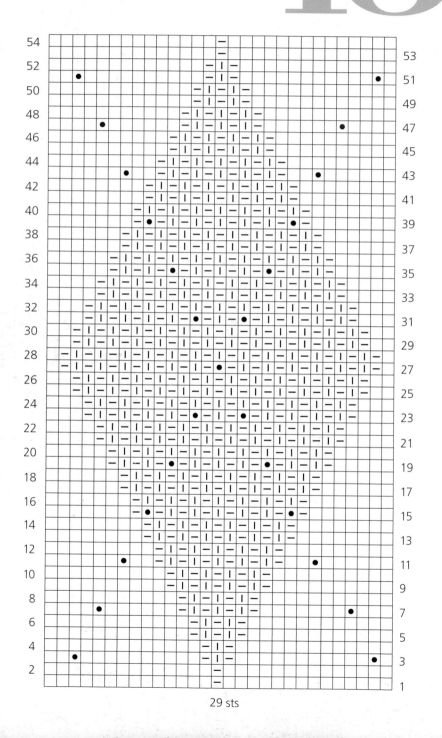

29 sts

Next row Work in seed st for 5 sts, k to last 5 sts, seed st 5 sts.
Next row Work in seed st for 5 sts, p to last 5 sts, seed st 5 sts.
Last 6 rows Work in seed st over all sts. Bind off in purl.

SCARF BODY
Cast on 39 sts. Work in seed st until piece measures 8"/20.5cm from beg, increasing 1 st on last WS row by kf&b in last st—40 sts.

BEGIN BASKETWEAVE SECTION
Rep rows 1–8 of basketweave st until basketweave section measures 48"/122cm, decreasing 1 st on last WS row by k2tog at end of row—39 sts. Work in seed st for 8"/20.5cm. Bind off in pat.

Finishing
Lightly block pieces to finished measurements.
With wrong side of pocket panel facing right side of scarf, sew sides and lower edge of each pocket panel to ends of scarf, using overcast stitch. ■

Stitch Key

☐ K on RS, p on WS

— P on RS, k on WS

Ⅰ K on RS, p on WS

● MB (Make Bobble)

17

Cabled Mittens

Twist your way through these heavily cabled mittens with a ribbed and shaped cuff.
Knit in a bright orange shade, these cozy mitts will warm your heart and hands.

DESIGNED BY LINDA MEDINA

Size
Instructions are written for one size.

Knitted Measurements
Hand circumference 7.5"/19cm
Length 10"/25.5cm

Materials
- 2 1¾oz/50g hanks (each approx 164yd/150m) of *Cascade 220 Sport* (Peruvian highland wool) in #7824 burnt orange
- One pair size 4 (3.5mm) needles *or size to obtain gauge*
- One set (5) size 4 (3.5mm) double-pointed needles (dpns)
- Stitch markers
- 2 1"/2.5cm buttons
- Stitch holder or smooth waste yarn in contrast color
- Cable needle (cn)

Note
Mitten cuff is worked back and forth in rows with short row shaping. Then hand of mitten is picked up along the shorter horizontal edge of the cuff and worked in the round.'

Stitch Glossary
Pfb Purl into the front and back of the next st to inc 1.
11-st RC Sl 6 sts to cn and hold to back, k2, p1, k2, then [p1, k2] twice from cn. Drop st, then yo Drop the next st and allow it to ladder down, then yo with working yarn.

Short Row
Wrap & Turn (w&t)
[on RS row (on WS row)]
1) Wyib (wyif), sl next st purlwise.
2) Move yarn between the needles to the front (back).
3) Sl the same st back to LH needle. Turn work. One st is wrapped.
4) When working the wrapped st, insert RH needle under the wrap and work it tog with the corresponding st on needle.

Right Mitten
CUFF
Cast on 20 sts on straight needles.
Row 1 (RS) P1, *k2, p2; rep from * to last st, p1.
Row 2 K1, *p2, k2; rep from * to last st, k1.
Rep rows 1 and 2 for cuff pat until piece measures 2¼"/5.5cm from beg, end with a WS row. Place marker at beg of last row.
BEG SHORT ROW SHAPING
*Short row 1 Cont in cuff pat, work 10 sts, w&t, work back in pat.
Short row 2 Work 5 sts in cuff pat, w&t, work back in pat.
Work 2 rows over all sts.
Rep short rows 1 and 2 once more.*
Work in cuff pat until piece measures 4"/10cm from marker, end with a WS row. Place marker at beg of last row. Rep from * to *.

Cont in cuff pat over all sts until piece measures 2¾"/7cm from 2nd marker, end with a WS row.

Gauge
38 sts and 27 rows to 4"/10cm over cable pat using size 4 (3.5mm) needles.
Take time to check gauge.

Cabled Mittens

END SHAPING

Dec row 1 (RS) K2tog tbl, work in pat to last 2 sts, k2tog—18 sts.

Dec row 2 (WS) P2tog tbl, work to last 2 sts, p2tog—16 sts.

Rep dec rows 1 and 2 once more, then dec row 1 once—10 sts.

Next row P2tog, bind off in pat to last 2 sts, p2tog, bind off last st.

Fold cuff at markers along short row shaping, overlapping shaped end over cast-on end at front. Pin in place, then sew overlapping ends tog.

HAND

Beg at outside edge marker, with RS facing and dpn #1 pick up and k 20 sts along first half of cuff edge, going through both layers of overlap; with dpn #2 pick up and k 19 sts to next marker; with dpn #3 pick up and k 20 sts for first half of back edge; with dpn #4 pick up and k 19 sts—78 sts. Remove cuff markers and pm for beg of rnd.

BEG CHART

Next (set-up) rnd Work set-up rnd of chart 3 times around.

Next 2 rnds Work rnds 1 and 2 of chart 3 times around.

THUMB GUSSET

Next (inc) rnd Work chart rnd 3 over 39 sts, pm, [pfb] twice, pm, cont in chart pat around.

Next rnd Work chart rnd 4 to next marker, sl marker, p to next marker, sl marker, cont in chart pat around.

Next (inc) rnd Work in chart pat to next marker, sl marker, pfb, p to 1 st before next marker, pfb, sl marker, cont in chart pat around.

Cont to work chart in this manner and rep inc rnd every other rnd 7 times more—20 p sts between markers.

Next rnd Work in pat to first marker, remove marker, p19, sl last 18 sts to scrap yarn or stitch holder for thumb, p1, remove next marker, cont in pat around.

Cont in chart pat until 24 rnds of chart are complete. Rep rnds 1–24 once more.

TOP SHAPING

Keeping beg of rnd as marked, arrange sts on dpns as foll: 20 sts on dpn #1; 19 sts on dpn #2; 20 sts on dpn #3; 19 sts on dpn #4.

Next (dec) rnd *P2, k2tog, cont in pat to last 4 sts on dpn #2, k2tog, k2; rep from * on needles 3 and 4.

Rep dec rnd every rnd until 18 sts rem. Cut yarn, leaving a 15"/38cm tail. Thread tail into yarn needle and run through remaining sts twice and draw up tightly.

THUMB

Place 18 thumb sts on 2 dpns. Rejoin yarn, p18, pick up and k 3 sts along edge of opening. Divide work evenly on 3 needles, pm for beg of rnd. Work in rev St st (p every rnd) until thumb measures 1¾"/4.5cm from picked-up sts.

THUMB SHAPING

Rnd 1 *P2tog, p5; rep from * around—18 sts.

Rnd 2 *P2tog, p4; rep from * around—15 sts.

Rnd 3 *P2tog, p3; rep from * around—12 st.

Rnd 4 *P2tog, p2; rep from * around—9 sts.

Rnd 5 *P2tog, p1; rep from * around—6 sts.

Cut yarn, leaving an 8"/20.5cm tail and thread into yarn needle. Run through remaining sts twice and draw up tightly. Sew button in place.

Left Mitten

CUFF

Work same as for right cuff, only beg short rows on WS rows.

HAND

Work same as for right mitten to thumb gusset, only beg pick-up at inside edge marker.

THUMB GUSSET

Next (inc) rnd [Pfb] twice, pm, work rnd 3 of chart pat 3 times around.

Next rnd P to next marker, sl marker, cont in chart pat around

Next (inc) rnd Pfb, p to st before next marker, pfb, sl marker, cont in chart pat around.

Cont to work chart in this manner and rep inc rnd every other rnd 7 times more—20 p sts between markers.

Next rnd P19, sl last 18 sts to scrap yarn or stitch holder for thumb, p1, remove next marker, cont in pat around.

Complete as for right mitten. ■

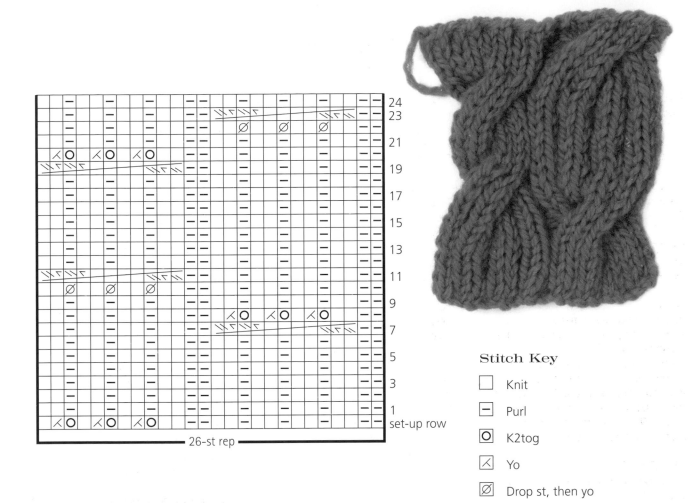

					24
					23
					21
					19
					17
					15
					13
					11
					9
					7
					5
					3
					1
					set-up row

◀ 26-st rep ▶

Stitch Key

☐	Knit
━	Purl
⊙	K2tog
⟋	Yo
⊘	Drop st, then yo

11-st RC

18 Checkerboard Hat

This duotone checkerboard hat is worked in intarsia with multiple bobbins going at once. You'll proclaim "checkmate" as you sew up the back seam!

DESIGNED BY THERESA SCHABES

Size
Instructions are written for one size.

Knitted Measurements
Head circumference 20"/51cm
Depth 7"/18cm

Materials
■ 1 1¾oz/50g hank (each approx 164yd/150m) of *Cascade 220 Sport* (Peruvian highland wool) each in #8622 camel (A) and #4002 jet (B)

■ One pair each sizes 7 and 8 (4.5 and 5mm) needles *or size to obtain gauge*

■ Bobbins

Notes
1) Use a double strand of yarn throughout.
2) Use a separate bobbin of color for each color section.
3) Wind 6 bobbins with double strand of A, 6 bobbins with double strand of B and 6 bobbins with 1 strand each of A and B for color C.
4) When changing colors, pick up new color from under dropped color to prevent holes.

Hat
With smaller needles and 2 strands of A held tog, cast on 86 sts.
Next row (RS) K3, *p2, k2; rep from *, end p3. Rep this row 7 times more, end with a WS row. Change to larger needles.

BEG CHART PAT
Row 1 (RS) Work first st, work 14-st rep 6 times, work last st. Cont to foll chart in this way to row 35—14 sts.
Next (dec) row (WS) With first bobbin of C, [p2tog] 7 times—7 sts. Cut all other bobbins, except this bobbin of C. Cut C leaving 20"/51cm tails and thread through rem sts. Pull tog tightly, secure end. Cut B, then using 1 strand of A, sew back seam. ■

Color Key
☐ 2 strands Camel (A)

■ 2 strands Jet (B)

▨ 1 strand Camel and 1 strand Jet (C)

Stitch Key
☐ K on RS, p on WS

◩ K2tog

▨ No stitch

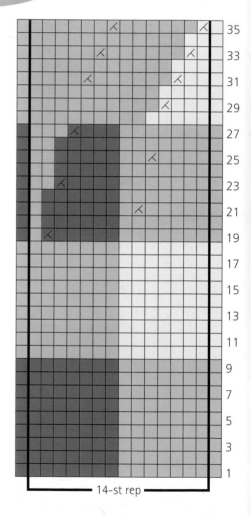

14-st rep

Gauge
17 sts and 24 rows to 4"/10cm over St st using double strand of yarn and larger needles. *Take time to check gauge.*

Lace-Panel Scarf

Knit in an elegant cream-colored yarn, this graceful lace panel surrounded on all sides with seed stitch gives off a very Victorian vibe.

DESIGNED BY JUDY SUMNER

■◼◼◻

Size
Instructions are written for one size.

Knitted Measurements
Approx 5" x 64"/12.5cm x 162.5cm

Materials
■ 2 1¾oz/50g hanks (each approx 164yd/150m) of *Cascade 220 Sport* (Peruvian highland wool) in #8010 natural

■ One pair size 6 (4mm) needles *or size to obtain gauge*

■ Stitch markers

Seed Stitch
(over an even number of sts)
Row 1 (RS) *K1, p1; rep from * to end.
Row 2 K the purl sts and p the knit sts.
Rep row 2 for seed st.

Scarf
Cast-on 28 sts. Work in seed st for 7 rows.
Next row (WS) Work in seed st over first 5 sts, pm, cont in seed st over center 18 sts, pm, work in seed st over last 5 sts. Keeping 5 sts each side in seed st as established, work center 18 sts in lace pat as foll:
Row 1 (RS) P1, k1 tbl, p1, [yo, k2tog] twice, k2, yo, k3, yo, SK2P, yo, p1, k1 tbl, p1—29 sts.
Row 2 K1, p1 tbl, k1, purl to last 3 sts, k1, p1 tbl, k1.
Row 3 P1, k1 tbl, p1, [yo, k2tog] twice, k2, yo, k2tog, k2, yo, k1, yo, ssk, yo, p1, k1 tbl, p1—31 sts.
Row 4 Rep row 2.
Row 5 P1, k1 tbl, p1, yo, k2tog, yo, [k2tog] 3 times, k2, yo, k3, yo, ssk, yo, p1, k1 tbl, p1.
Row 6 Rep row 2.
Row 7 P1, k1 tbl, p1, yo, k2tog, [k3tog] twice, yo, k1, yo, k2, [ssk, yo] twice, p1, k1 tbl, p1—9 sts.

Row 8 K1, p1 tbl, k1, p9, p2tog, p2, k1, p1 tbl, k1—28 sts.
Row 9 P1, k1 tbl, p1, yo, k3tog, yo, k3, yo, k2, [ssk, yo] twice, p1, k1 tbl, p1—29 sts.
Row 10 Rep row 2.
Row 11 P1, k1 tbl, p1, yo, k2tog, yo, k1, yo, k2, ssk, yo, k2, [ssk, yo] twice, p1, k1 tbl, p1—31 sts.
Row 12 Rep row 2.
Row 13 P1, k1 tbl, p1, yo, k2tog, yo, k3, yo, k2, [ssk] 3 times, yo, ssk, yo, p1, k1 tbl, p1—31 sts
Row 14 Rep row 2.
Row 15 P1, k1 tbl, p1, [yo, k2tog] twice, k2, yo, k1, yo, [SK2P] twice, ssk, yo, p1, k1 tbl, p1—29 sts.
Row 16 K1, p1 tbl, k1, p2, p2tog, p9, k1, p1 tbl, k1—28 sts. Rep these 16 rows until piece measures 63"/160cm from beg, end with row 8 or 16, dropping markers. Cont in seed st for 8 rows. Bind off in seed st.

Finishing
Block piece lightly to measurements. ◼

Gauge
20 sts and 28 rows to 4"/10cm over St st using size 6 (4mm) needles. *Take time to check gauge.*

Cabled Ski Cap

Take a trip down a double black diamond trail in this bobbled-and-cabled hat. Knit in a bright pink with a contrasting brim-edge and pompom, it will be easy to spot as you fly down the hill.

DESIGNED BY YOKO HATTA

Size
Instructions are written for one size.

Knitted Measurements
Head circumference 21"/53.5cm

Materials
- 2 1¾oz/50g hanks (each approx 164yd/150m) of *Cascade 220 Sport* (Peruvian highland wool) in #7805 flamingo pink (MC)
- 1 1¾oz/50g hank (each approx 164yd/150m) of Cascade Yarns *220 Sport* (Peruvian highland wool) in #8400 charcoal grey (CC)
- One set (5) size 6 (4mm) double-pointed needles (dpns) *or size to obtain gauge*
- One set (5) size 4 (3.5mm) double-pointed needles (dpns)
- Stitch marker
- Cable needle (cn)
- 2"/5cm pompom maker

2X2 Rib
Rnd 1 P1, *k2, p2; rep from * to last st, p1.
Rep rnd 1 for pat.

Stitch Glossary
6-st LC Sl 3 sts to cn and hold to *front*, k3, k3 from cn.
4-st LC Sl 2 sts to cn and hold to *front*, k2, k2 from cn.
2-st LC Sl 1 st to cn and hold to *front*, k1, k1 from cn.
2-st RC Sl 1 st to cn and hold to *back*, k1, k1 from cn.
2-st LPC Sl 1 st to cn and hold to *front*, p1, k1 from cn.
2-st RPC Sl 1 st to cn and hold to *back*, k1, p1 from cn.

Hat
With smaller needles and CC, cast on 120 sts. Join and pm, taking care not to twist sts on needle. Work in 2X2 rib for 2 rnds. Change to MC and cont in rib pat for 40 rnds more. Change to larger needles.

Next (inc) rnd *P1, k2, p2, M1, k2, M1, p2, k2, p2, M1, k2, p2, k2, M1, p1; rep from * around—144 sts. Beg chart, working 6 repeats of chart around for 59 rnds—12 sts. Cut yarn, leaving an 8"/20.5cm tail and thread through rem sts. Pull tog tightly and secure end.

Finishing
Block piece lightly to measurements.

POMPOM
With CC, wrap yarn densely around a 2"/5cm pompom maker. Finish pompom following package directions. Sew pompom to center top of hat. ■

Quick Tip
For a different look, knit the hat using all one color of yarn or knit the entire ribbed band in a contrasting color.

Gauge
27 sts and 30 rows to 4"/10cm over chart pat using size 6 (4mm) needles. *Take time to check gauge.*

20 Cabled Ski Cap

Stitch Key

□	Knit
−	Purl
⟋ (K2tog symbol)	K2tog
⟍ (Ssk symbol)	Ssk
◺	P2tog
◿	P2tog tbl
⧅	2-st RC
⧅	2-st LC
⧄	2-st RPC
⧄	2-st LPC
⧄	4-st LC
⧄	6-st LC
▩	No stitch

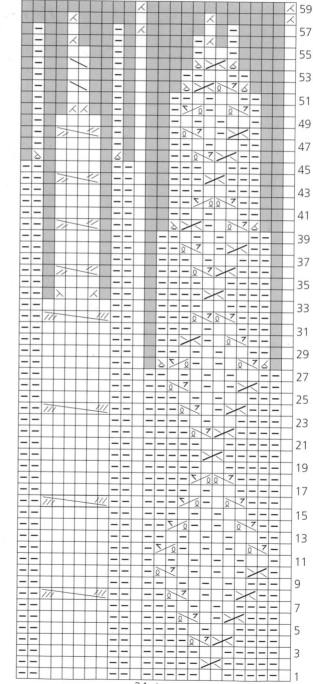

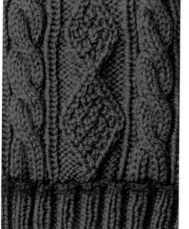

24 sts

Cable-Accent Fingerless Mitts

A twist on an everyday classic! An elegant braided cable marches up the center of these rib-trimmed fingerless mitts—the perfect pattern for a first-time cable knitter.

DESIGNED BY LORI STEINBERG

Size
Instructions are written for one size.

Knitted Measurements
Hand circumference 7"/18cm
Length of cuff Approx 1¼"/3cm

Materials
■ 1 1¾oz/50g hank (each approx 164yd/150m) of *Cascade 220 Sport* (Peruvian highland wool) in #2452 turtle

■ One set (5) size 4 (3.5mm) double-pointed needles (dpns) *or size to obtain gauge*

■ Cable needle (cn)

■ Stitch markers

Note
To work in the rnd, always read chart from right to left.

Stitch Glossary
4-st RC Sl 2 sts to cn and hold to *back*, k2, k2 from cn.
4-st LC Sl 2 sts to cn and hold to *front*, k2, k2 from cn.
kf&b Inc 1 by knitting into the front and back of the next st.
M1 p-st Insert LH needle from front to back under the strand between the last st worked and the next st. P through back loop to twist the st.

Gauge
26 sts and 34 rnds to 4"/10cm over St st using size 4 (3.5mm) dpns. *Take time to check gauge.*

Cable-Accent Fingerless Mitts

Right Mitt

CUFF
Cast on 48 sts. Divide sts over 4 needles. Join, taking care not to twist sts on needles, pm for beg of rnds. Cont in rib pat as foll:
Rnd 1 *K1, p2; rep from * around. Rep this rnd for 1¼"/3cm.
Next (set-up) rnd K7, p2, k3, kf&b, k3, p2, k to end of rnd—49 sts.

BEG CHART PAT
Rnd 1 K7, work rnd 1 of chart over next 12 sts, knit to end of rnd. Cont to foll chart in this way until piece measures 2¼"/5.5cm from beg.

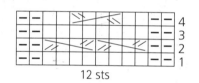

12 sts

Stitch Key

☐ Knit

⊟ Purl

4-st RC

4-st LC

THUMB GUSSET
Inc rnd 1 Work in pat as established over first 25 sts, M1 p-st, pm, k1, pm, M1 p-st, work to end of rnd—51 sts.
Next 3 rnds Work in pat as established, purling new (inc) sts.
Inc rnd 2 Work in pat as established to first marker, sl marker, M1, knit to next marker, M1, sl marker, work to end of rnd—53 sts.
Next 3 rnds Work in pat as established, knitting new (inc) sts. Rep last 4 rnds 6 times more—65 sts (15 sts between thumb gusset markers).
Next rnd Work to one st before first marker, place next 17 sts on scrap yarn for thumb (dropping markers), cast on 1 st, work to end of rnd—49 sts.

HAND
Work even in pat as established until piece measures 7"/18cm from beg, end with rnd 2 of chart.
Next rnd [K1, p2] 4 times, k2tog, p2, *k1, p2; rep from * to end of rnd—48 sts. Cont in k1, p2 rib for ¾"/2cm. Bind off in rib.

THUMB
Place 17 thumb gusset sts over 3 needles.
Next rnd Join yarn at inside of thumb, working along thumb opening, pick up and p 1 st, pick up and k 1 st, then pick up and p 1 st; working sts on dpns, p1, cont in k1, p2 rib to last st, M1, p1—21 sts. Join and pm for beg of rnds. Cont in rib pat as established for ¾"/2cm. Bind off knitwise.

Left Mitt
Work same as right mitt to thumb gusset.

THUMB GUSSET
Inc rnd 1 M1 p-st, pm, k1, pm, M1 p-st, work to end of rnd—51 sts.
Next 3 rnds Work in pat as established, purling new (inc) sts.
Inc rnd 2 P1, sl marker, M1, knit to next marker, M1, sl marker, work to end of rnd—53 sts.
Next 3 rnds Work in pat as established, knitting new (inc) sts. Rep last 4 rnds 6 times more—65 sts (15 sts between thumb gusset markers).
Next rnd Place first 17 sts on scrap yarn for thumb (dropping markers), cast on 1 st, work to end of rnd—49 sts. Cont to work same as right mitt to thumb.

THUMB
Place 17 thumb gusset sts over 3 needles.
Next rnd Join yarn at inside of thumb, working along thumb opening, pick up and p 1 st, pick up and k 1 st, then pick up and p 1 st; working sts on dpns, p1, M1, p2, cont in k1, p2 rib to last 2 sts, end k1 p1—21 sts. Join and pm for beg of rnds. Cont in rib pat as established for ¾"/2cm. Bind off knitwise. ■

22

Triangle Lace Scarf

Knit in a luscious lemon-yellow yarn, this lovely lace scarf is a sure attention-grabber. Two lace panels are knit separately then joined together.

DESIGNED BY ANASTASIA BLAES

Size
Instructions are written for one size.

Knitted Measurements
Approx 7½" x 60"/19.5cm x 152.5cm

Materials
■ 3 1¾oz/50g hanks (each approx 164yd/150m) of *Cascade 220 Sport* (Peruvian highland wool) in #4147 lemon yellow

■ One pair size 6 (4mm) needles *or size to obtain gauge*

■ Spare size 6 (4mm) needle (for 3-needle bind-off)

■ Stitch markers

Note
Scarf is made in two panels, then joined in the center using 3-needle bind-off.

Panels (make 2)
Cast on 41 sts. Knit 4 rows. Purl next row. Cont in triangle lace st as foll:

BEG CHART PAT
Row 1 (RS) K2, pm, work 6-st rep 5 times, work last 7 sts, pm, k2.

Row 2 K2, sl marker, work first 7 sts, work 6-st rep 5 times, sl marker, k2. Keeping 2 sts each side in garter st (knit every row), cont to foll chart in this way to row 20, then rep rows 1–20 9 times more, then rows 1–19 once. Leave sts on needle.

Finishing
With RS facing, hold panels tog on two parallel needles. Using third needle, work 3-needle bind-off. Block piece lightly to measurements. ■

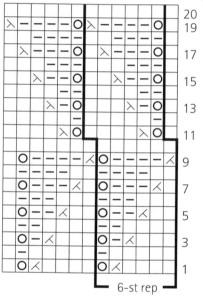

6-st rep

Stitch Key

☐	K on RS, p on WS
—	P on RS, k on WS
Ｏ	Yarn over
⟋	K2tog
⟍	Ssk

Gauge
22 sts and 30 rows to 4"/10cm over chart pat using size 6 (4mm) needles.
Take time to check gauge.

23
Tasseled Fair Isle Hat

Frightened of Fair Isle? Face your fears head-on with a simple square hat with zero shaping. You'll get the hang of colorwork in no time.

DESIGNED BY HEIDI TODD KOZAR

Size
Instructions are written for one size.

Knitted Measurements
Head circumference 20"/51cm
Depth 8"/20.5cm

Materials
■ 1 1¾oz/50g hank (each approx 164yd/150m) of *Cascade 220 Sport* (Peruvian highland wool) each in #2453 pumpkin spice (A), #8555 black (B) and #9408 cordovan (C)

■ Sizes 4 and 5 (3.5 and 3.75mm) circular needles, 16"/40cm long *or size to obtain gauge*

■ Spare size 5 (3.75cm) circular needle

■ Two size 4 (3.5mm) double-pointed needles (dpns) for I-cords

■ Stitch marker

Note
To work in the rnd, always read chart from right to left.

Stitch Glossary
kf&b Inc 1 by knitting into the front and back of the next st.

Hat
With smaller circular needle and A, cast on 114 sts. Join and pm, taking care not to twist sts on needle. Work in St st (knit every rnd) for 3"/7.5cm.
Next (turning ridge) rnd Purl.
Next (inc) rnd *K18, kf&b; rep from * around—120 sts. Change to larger needle.

BEG CHART PAT
Rnd 1 Work 20-st rep 6 times. Cont to foll chart in this way to rnd 52.

Finishing
Place first 60 sts on spare larger needle. Using Kitchener st, graft top seam tog using B. Fold bottom edge to WS along turning ridge and sew in place using A.

Gauge
24 sts and 28 rnds to 4"/10cm over St st and chart pat using larger circular needle.
Take time to check gauge.

23 Tasseled Fair Isle Hat

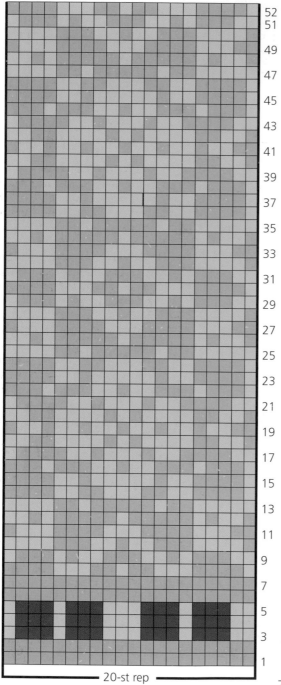

52
51
49
47
45
43
41
39
37
35
33
31
29
27
25
23
21
19
17
15
13
11
9
7
5
3
1

20-st rep

POMPOM CORDS (MAKE 2)

With dpn and B, cast on 4 sts, leaving a long tail for sewing. Work in I-cord as foll: *__Next row (RS)__ With 2nd dpn, k4, _do not turn._ Slide sts back to beg of needle to work next row from RS; rep from * for 3"/7.5cm. Cut yarn, leaving a 6"/15cm tail and thread through rem sts. Pull tog tightly, secure end, then sew to one corner of hat.

POMPOMS (MAKE 2)

With B and C, make a 2½"/6.5cm diameter pompom (see page 75). Sew pompoms to pompom cords. ■

Color Key

☐ Pumpkin Spice (A)

▨ Black (B)

▧ Cordovan (C)

Striped Earflap Hat

Grab your five favorite colors and start striping! Required wearing for extra-cold weather, an earflap hat is flattering on everyone.

DESIGNED BY JACQUELINE VAN DILLEN

Size

Instructions are written for one size.

Knitted Measurements

Head circumference 22"/56cm

Materials

■ 1 1¾oz/50g hank (each approx 164yd/150m) of *Cascade 220 Sport* (Peruvian highland wool) each in #7822 vandyke brown (MC), #8914 granny smith (A), #9430 highland green (B), #9421 blue hawaii (C), #8910 citron (D)

■ One pair size 3 (3.25mm) needles *or size to obtain gauge*

■ Crochet hook (for attaching braids)

■ 2½"/ 6.5cm pompom maker

Hat

Cast on 126 sts with MC. Work St st (knit on RS, purl on WS) for 11 rows.
Switch to C and k 2 rows.
Switch to A and k 1 row, then work 11 rows in St st.
Switch to MC and k 2 rows.
Switch to C and k 1 row and then work 11 rows in St st.

Switch to MC and k 2 rows.
Switch to D and k 1 row and then work 11 rows in St st.
Switch to MC and k 2 rows.
Switch to B and k 1 row and then work 11 rows in St st. AT THE SAME TIME, after 4 rows B start crown shaping on RS rows only:
*K 19 sts, k2tog; rep from * to end of rnd.
*K 18 sts, k2tog; rep from * to end of rnd.
*K 17 sts, k2tog; rep from * to end of rnd.
*K 16 sts, k2tog; rep from * to end of rnd.
Switch to D and k 2 rows.
Switch to MC and k 1 row and cont in St st. AT THE SAME TIME, cont with crown shaping on RS rows only:
*K 15 sts, k2tog; rep from * to end of rnd.
*K 14 sts, k2tog; rep from * to end of rnd.
*K 13 sts, k2tog; rep from * to end of rnd.
*K 12 sts, k2tog; rep from * to end of rnd.
K2tog,*k10, k3tog; rep from * four times, end k9, k2tog—66sts.
K2tog,*k8, k3tog; rep from * four times, end k7, k2tog.
K2tog,*k6, k3tog; rep from * four times, end k5, k2tog.
K2tog,*k4, k3tog; rep from * four times, end k3, k2tog.
K2tog,*k2, k3tog; rep from * four times, end k1, k2tog.

Gauge

22 sts and 30 rows to 4"/10cm over St st using size 3 (3.25mm) needles.
Take time to check gauge.

Striped Earflap Hat

Next RS row K2tog; rep to end—9 sts.
Cut yarn, leaving long tails.
Thread needle with yarn tails and draw through the last 9 sts tightly, being careful not to break yarn.
With MC, pick up 124 sts evenly around the brim. K 3 rows.
Row 4 Bind off 14 sts, k26, bind off 44 sts, k26, bind off 14 sts.

EARFLAPS (work one at a time)
K every row until earflap measures 3.25"/8cm.
Bind off 1 st at the beg of next 6 rows, 2 sts at the beg of next 4 rows, and 4 sts at beg of next 3 rows.

Finishing

Sew back seam of hat. Block lightly to measurements.

Make 2 braids with all colors (20"/50cm long) and attach to the end of each earflap.

BRAIDS (MAKE 2)
Cut strands from each color that are twice the desired length (plus extra for knotting). On the WS of the bottom of the earflap, insert crochet hook from front to back through the earflap and over the folded yarn. Pull yarn through and tighten. Make a braid (6, 7 and 7 threads). Tie a knot and trim to create a fringe.

POMPOM
With all five colors, make a pompom using a 2½"/6.5cm pompom maker or instructions below. Sew pompom to center top of hat. ■

HOW TO MAKE A POMPOM

1. Cut a center hole in two circular pieces of cardboard the width of the desired pompom. Then cut a pie-shaped wedge out of each circle.

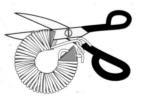

2. Hold the two circles together and wrap the yarn tightly around the cardboard. Carefully cut around the cardboard.

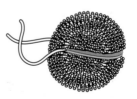

3. Tie a piece of yarn tightly between the two circles. Remove the cardboard and trim the pompom. Hold the two circles together and wrap the yarn tightly around the cardboard. Then carefully cut around the cardboard.

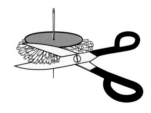

4. Sandwich the pompom between two round pieces of cardboard held together with a long needle. Cut around the circumference for a perfect pompom.

Garter Hood with Lace Edging

A touch of lace brings a touch of class to this elegant hood-style scarf. Worked primarily in garter stitch, the hood is created by seaming up a portion of the back.

DESIGNED BY EDNA HART

Size
Instructions are written for one size.

Knitted Measurements
Hood 10½"/26.5cm deep x10½"/ 26.5cm high (excluding scarf ties)
Length 27"/68.5cm (including scarf ties)

Materials
■ 3 1¾oz/50g hanks (each approx 164yd/150m) of *Cascade 220 Sport* (Peruvian highland wool) in #7803 magenta

■ One pair size 8 (5mm) needles *or size to obtain gauge*

■ Stitch markers

■ Size G/6 (4mm) crochet hook

Ostrich Plume Stitch
(worked over 13 sts)
Row 1 (RS) K13.
Row 2 P13.
Row 3 K4tog, [yo, k1] 5 times, yo, k4tog.
Row 4 P13.
Rep rows 1–4 for ostrich plume st.

Hood
LEFT SCARF TIE
Cast on 19 sts. Work in garter st (knit every row) for 4 rows.

Row 1 (RS) K3, pm, work row 1 of ostrich plume st over next 13 sts, pm, k3.
Row 2 K3, sl marker, work row 2 of ostrich plume st over next 13 sts, sl marker, k3.
Row 3 K3, sl marker, work row 3 of ostrich plume st over next 13 sts, sl marker, k3.
Row 4 K3, sl marker, work row 4 of ostrich plume st over next 13 sts, sl marker, k3.
Next (inc) row (RS) K1, M1, k2, sl marker, work row 1 of ostrich plume st over next 13 sts, sl marker, k3—20 sts. Keeping sts between markers in ostrich plume st as established, and sts each side in garter st, cont to inc 1 st at same edge every 3rd row 31 times more—51 sts. Piece should measure approx 16½"/42cm from beg. Mark beg and end of last row for beg of hood.

Hood
Work even until piece measures 21"/53.5cm above marked row, end with a WS row. Mark beg and end of last row for end of hood.

Gauge
20 sts and 36 rows to 4"/10cm over garter st using size 8 (5mm) needles.
Take time to check gauge.

Garter Hood with Lace Edging

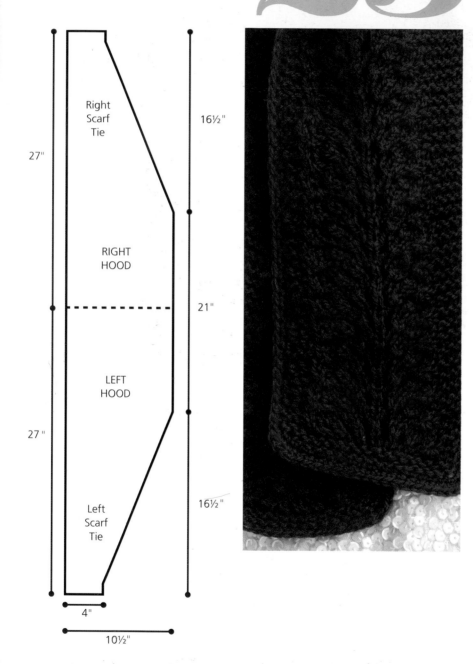

Right
Scarf
Tie

27"

16½"

RIGHT
HOOD

21"

LEFT
HOOD

27"

16½"

Left
Scarf
Tie

4"

10½"

RIGHT SCARF TIE
Next (dec) row (RS) K1, k2tog, k to marker, sl marker, work in ostrich plume st over next 13 sts, sl marker, k3—50 sts. Cont to dec 1 st at same edge every 3rd row 31 times more, end with a WS row—19 sts. Work even for 4 rows, dropping markers on last row. Work in garter st for 4 rows. Bind off knitwise.

Finishing
Block piece to measurements. Fold piece in half. Sew back seam of hood for 10½"/26.5cm.

EDGING
With RS facing and crochet hook, join yarn with a sl st in bottom of back seam.
Rnd 1 (RS) Ch 1, sc evenly around entire outer edge, working 3 sc in each corner, join rnd with a sl st in first st.
Rnd 2 Ch 1, sc in each st around, working 3 sc in each corner st, join rnd with a sl st in first sc. Fasten off. ■

Textured Earflap Hat

You'll stop traffic and turn heads in this bright orange cap. With its dense textured pattern and earflaps, it will keep you toasty warm.

DESIGNED BY LORI STEINBERG

Size
Instructions are written for one size.

Knitted Measurements
Head circumference 20"/51cm
Depth 6½"/16.5cm (excluding earflaps)

Materials
■ 3 1¾oz/50g hanks (each approx 164yd/150m) of *Cascade 220 Sport* (Peruvian highland wool) in #7825 orange sherbet

■ One pair size 4 (3.5mm) needles *or size to obtain gauge*

■ Spare size 4 (3.5mm) needle

■ Size 4 (3.5mm) circular needle, 16"/40cm long

■ One set (5) size 4 (3.5mm) double–pointed needles (dpns)

■ Size G/6 (4mm) crochet hook

■ Stitch markers

Notes
1) When working in rows, read chart from right to left on RS rows and from left to right on WS rows.
2) When working in rnds, always read chart from right to left.

Hat
FIRST EARFLAP
With straight needles, cast on 14 sts.
Set up row (WS) K3, p2, k4, p2, k3.
BEG CHART PAT
Row 1 (RS) P3, sl 2 wyib, p4, sl 2 wyib, p3.
Row 2 K3, p2, k4, p2, k3.

Gauge
28 sts and 54 rnds to 4"/10cm over chart pat using size 4 (3.5mm) circular needle. *Take time to check gauge.*

Textured Earflap Hat

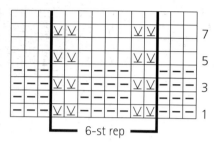

6-st rep

Stitch Key

☐ K on RS, p on WS

⊟ P on RS, k on WS

V̲ Slip 1 wyib

Inc row (RS) Inc 1 st in first st, work to last st, inc 1 st in last st—16 sts. Working inc sts into pat, rep inc row every alternate 4th and 2nd row 3 times more—28 sts. Cont to rep inc row every other row 10 times, end with a WS row—48 sts. Cast on 2 sts at beg of next 12 rows, end with a WS row—72 sts. Cut yarn. Leave sts on spare needle. Set aside.

SECOND EARFLAP

Work same as first earflap. *Do not cut yarn.* With circular needle, cont as foll:
Next rnd (RS) Cont in pat over 72 sts of second earflap, then cont in pat over 72 sts of first earflap, join to work in the rnd and work next 2 sts, pm for beg of rnds—144 sts. Work even in chart pat over all sts until piece measures 3½"/9cm from joining rnd, end with row 8.

CROWN SHAPING

Change to dpns (dividing sts evenly between 4 needles) when there are too few sts on circular needle.
Dec rnd 1 [Sl 2, p2tog, p2, sl 2, p4] 12 times—132 sts. Cont in pat as established for 3 rnds.
Dec rnd 2 [Sl 2, k3, sl 2, k1, k2tog, k1] 12 times—120 sts. Cont in pat as established for 3 rnds.
Dec rnd 3 [Sl 2, p2tog, p1, sl 2, p3] 12 times—108 sts. Cont in pat as established for 3 rnds.

Dec rnd 4 [Sl 2, k2, sl 2, k2tog, k1] 12 times—96 sts. Cont in pat as established for 11 rnds (working pat with 2 k sts or 2 p sts between sl st ribs).
Dec rnd 5 [K2tog] 48 times—48 sts. K next rnd.
Dec rnd 6 [K2tog] 24 times—24 sts. K next rnd.
Dec rnd 7 [K2tog] 12 times—12 sts. Cut yarn leaving an 8"/20.5cm tail and thread through rem sts. Pull tog tightly and secure end.

Finishing
EDGING
With RS facing and crochet hook, join yarn with a sl st in center back edge. Making sure that edge lies flat, sl st around entire bottom edge, join rnd with a sl st in first st. Fasten off. With WS facing, circular needle and working through front lps of sl sts, pick up and k 3 sts for every 4 sl sts. Bind off kwise.

TIES (MAKE 2)
Cut fifteen 16"/40.5cm long strands of yarn. Hold strands tog and fold in half. Tie off securely ½"/1cm below fold. Divide strands into three groups of 10 strands. Braid for 8"/20.5cm. Tie off firmly to secure braid. Trim strands evenly, 2"/5cm below last tie-off. On WS, sew folded edge of braid to center bottom of earflap. Make a 4"/10cm-diameter pompom. Sew to top of hat. ■

27

Multi-Lace Scarf

Featuring two lace patterns and a cluster stitch, this lovely neck warmer
would make a wonderful gift for any lace lover.

DESIGNED BY ANNA AL

Size
Instructions are written for one size.

Knitted Measurements
Approx 6½" x 86"/16.5cm x 218.5cm

Materials
- 4 1¾oz/50g hanks (each approx 164yd/150m) of *Cascade 220 Sport* (Peruvian highland wool) in #8010 natural
- One pair size 6 (4mm) needles *or size to obtain gauge*
- Stitch markers

Stitch Glossary
Cluster stitch Pass 3rd st on LH needle over first and 2nd sts, then k1, yo, k1 over these 2 sts.

Scarf
Cast on 44 sts.

BEG CHART PAT I
Row 1 (RS) Work first 6 sts, pm, work 4-st rep 8 times, pm, work last 6 sts. Slipping markers every row, rep rows 1 and 2 until piece measures 5"/12.5cm from beg, end with row 1.
Row (inc) 2 (WS) Work first 6 sts, sl marker, M1, work to end—45 sts.

BEG CHART PAT II
Row 1 (RS) Work first 6 sts as established, sl marker, work 16-st rep twice, work last st, sl marker, work last 6 sts as established. Cont to foll chart in this way to row 26, then rep rows 1–26 until piece measures approx 81"/205.5cm from beg, ending with row 9.
Row (dec) 10 (WS) Work first 6 sts as established, sl marker, p2tog tbl, work to end—44 sts.

BEG CHART PAT I
Row 1 (RS) Work first 6 sts, sl marker, work 4-st rep 8 times, sl marker, work last 6 sts. Cont to foll chart in this way to row 2, then rep rows 1 and 2 until piece measures 86"/218.5cm from beg, end with row 2. Bind off kwise.

Finishing
Block piece lightly to measurements. ■

Gauge
27 sts and 32 rows to 4"/10cm over chart pats using size 6 (4mm) needles (after blocking).
Take time to check gauge.

Multi-Lace Scarf

CHART I

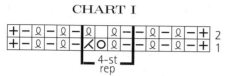

4-st
rep

2
1

CHART II

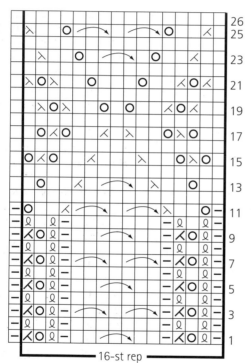

26
25
23
21
19
17
15
13
11
9
7
5
3
1

— 16-st rep —

Stitch Key

☐ K on RS, p on WS

— P on RS, K on WS

＋ K on RS, K on WS

ℓ K1 tbl on RS, p1 tbl on WS

Ｏ Yarn over

╱ K2tog

╲ Ssk

╱ K2tog tbl

Cluster stitch

Floral-Motif Scarf

Create your own secret garden with this flower- and leaf-motif scarf.
Set on a background of reverse stockinette and bordered on both ends with
dainty leaves, it evokes the lushness of fresh foliage.

DESIGNED BY JACQUELINE JEWETT

Size

Instructions are written for one size.

Knitted Measurements

Approx 6" x 62" / 15cm x 157.5 cm
(excluding leaf fringe)

Materials

■ 3 1¾oz/50g hanks (each approx
164yd/150m) of *Cascade 220 Sport*
(Peruvian highland wool) each in
#2452 turtle

■ One pair size 6 (4mm) needles *or
size to obtain gauge*

■ Cable needle

Stitch Glossary

2-st RT Sl 1 st to cn and hold to *back,*
k1, k1 from cn.

2-st LT Sl 1 st to cn and hold to *front,* k1,
k1 from cn.

K1B Knit through back loop.

FPC (Front P Cross) Sl 2 k sts to cn and
hold to *front,* p1, k2 from cn.

BPC (Back P Cross) Sl 1 p st to cn and
hold to *back,* k2, p 1 from cn.

FDKC (Front Double K Cross) Sl 2 k sts
to cn and hold to *front,* k2, k2 from cn.

BDKC (Back Double K Cross) Sl 2 k sts
to cn and hold to *back,* k2, k2 from cn.

MB (make bobble) (K1, k1B, k1, k1B, k1)
into next st. Turn, p5, turn, k5, turn,
P2tog, p1, p2tog, turn, k3tog, pick up
and k 1 st from base of st, sl previously
made st over this one to anchor bobble.

Scarf

Cast on 36 sts. K 4 rows.

Row 5 K2, 2-st RT, *p4, k4; rep from *
twice, p4, 2-st LT, k2.

Row 6 and all WS rows K the k sts,
p the p sts (unless otherwise noted).
Also, k the first 2 sts and last 2 sts
of all WS rows.

Rows 7 and 9 Rep row 5.

Row 11 K2, 2-st RT, *k4, p4;
rep from * twice, k4, 2-st LT, k2—36 sts.

Rows 13 and 15 Rep row 11.

Rows 17, 19, 21 Rep row 5.

Row 23 K2, 2-st RT, p12, BDKC, p12,
2-st LT, k2.

Rows 25 and 27 K2, 2-st RT, p12, k4,
p12, 2-st LT, k2.

Rows 29–40 Rep rows 23–28 twice.

Row 41 Rep row 23.

Row 43 K2, 2-st RT, p11, BPC, FPC,
p11, 2-st LT, k2—36 sts.

Gauge

24 sts and 28 rows to 4"/10cm over pat st using size 6 (4mm) needles. *Take time to check gauge.*

28

Floral-Motif Scarf

Row 44 K2, P2 , k11, p2, k1, M1, k1, p2, k11, P2, k2—37 sts.

Row 45 K2, 2-st RT, p10, BPC, p1, MB, p1, FPC, p10, 2-st LT, k2.

Row 47 K2, 2-st RT, p9, BPC, p5, FPC, p9, 2-st LT, k2.

Row 49 K2, 2-st RT, p8, BPC, MB, p2, MB, p2, MB, FPC, p8, 2-st LT, k2.

Row 51 K2, 2-st RT, p8, FPC, p7, BPC, p8, 2-st LT, k2.

Row 53 K2, 2-st RT, p9, FPC, p2, MB, p2, BPC, p9, 2-st LT, k2.

Row 55 K2, 2-st RT, p10, FPC, p3, BPC, P10, 2-st LT, k2.

Row 57 K2, 2-st RT, p11 FPC, place next 2 p sts on cn and hold to back, k2, p2tog from cn, p11, 2-st LT, k2—36 sts.

Row 59 K2, 2-st RT, p 12, FDKC, p12, 2-st LT, k2.

Rows 61 and 63 Rep row 25.

Rows 65–76 Rep rows 59–64 twice more.

Row 77 Rep row 59.

Row 79 K2, 2-st RT, p11, BPC, FPC, p11, 2-st LT, k2.

Row 80 Rep row 44—37 sts.

Row 81 K2, 2-st RT, p10, BPC, p3, FPC, p10, 2-st LT, k2.

Row 83 K2, 2-st RT, p9, BPC, P2, MB, P2, FPC, P9, 2-st LT, k2.

Row 85 K2, 2-st RT, p9, FPC, P5, BPC, p9, 2-st LT, k2.

Row 87 K2, 2-st RT, p10, FPC, p3, BPC, p10, 2-st LT, k2.

Row 89 K2, 2-st RT, p11, FPC, place next 2 sts on to cn and hold to back, k2, p2tog from cn, p11, 2-st LT, k2—36 sts.

Row 90 Rep row 6.

Rep rows 23–90 four times more, then rows 23–59 once (6 large diamonds and 5 small diamonds).

Last 36 rows Work rows 5–40 in reverse order (reversing cable on row 23). k 4 rows. Cast off 36 sts.

Flower Petals (make 66)

Cast on 1 st, turn, p1, turn, k into front, back & front to make 3 sts. Turn, p3, turn, k1, yo, k1, yo, k1,turn, p5, turn, k2, yo, k1, yo, k2, turn, p7, turn, k3, yo, k1, yo, k3, turn, p9, turn, k3, SKP, then sl next st over this st, k3, turn, p7, turn k2, rep as before for next 3 sts. p2, turn, p5, turn, p1, next 3 as before, p1, turn, p3, turn, work 3 as before. Break yarn leaving about a 12"/30.5cm thread for sewing onto scarf.

Finishing

Sew in all ends, attach flower petals as foll: 6 petals around each large diamond and 1 petal on either side of each small diamond. On short edges of scarf sew 1 leaf/petal over each of the 5 k stripes, starting where the garter rows edging meets the k4 p4 patterns. Add 5 leaves on reverse side to correspond. Sew the leaf sides tog to secure. ■

Slip-Stitch Mittens

Switch up your color choice to personalize these gender-neutral mitts. Make them bold and bright or keep things simple with a tone-on-tone color scheme.

DESIGNED BY MARY BETH TEMPLE

Size
Instructions are written for one size.

Knitted measurements
Hand circumference 7"/17.5cm
Length of cuff Approx 2¾"/7cm.

Materials
■ 1 1¾oz/50g hank (each approx 164yd/150m) of *Cascade 220 Sport* (Peruvian highland wool) each in #8886 italian plum (A) and #2450 mystic purple (B)

■ One set (4) each sizes 3 and 4 (3.25 and 3.5mm) double-pointed needles (dpns) *or size to obtain gauge*

■ Stitch markers

Stitch Glossary
kf&b Inc 1 by knitting into the front and back of the next st.

Slip Stitch Pattern
(multiple of 3 sts)
Rnd 1 With B, *k2, sl 1; rep from * around.
Rnd 2 With B, knit. **Rnd 3** With A, *sl 1, k2; rep from * around. **Rnd 4** With A, knit.
Rep rnds 1–4 for slip st pat.

Mitten (make 2)
CUFF
With smaller dpns and A, cast on 38 sts.

Divide sts over 3 needles. Join, taking care not to twist sts on needles, pm for beg of rnds. Cont in k1, p1 rib for 2½"/6.5cm. Change to larger dpns.
Next (inc) rnd Knit, inc 2 sts evenly spaced around—40 sts. Cont in slip st pat and work thumb gusset as foll:

THUMB GUSSET
Rnd 1 With B, k1, pm, kf&b, pm, k1, sl 1, *k2, sl 1; rep from * to end—41 sts. **Rnd 2** With B, knit. **Rnd 3** With A, sl 1, sl marker, [kf&b] twice, sl marker, k2, *sl 1, k2; rep from * to end—43 sts. **Rnd 4** With A, knit. **Rnd 5** With B, k 1, sl marker, k to next marker, sl marker, k1, sl 1, *k2, sl 1; rep from * to end. **Rnd 6** With B, knit. **Rnd 7** With A, sl 1, sl marker, kf&b, knit to st before next marker, kf&b, sl marker, k2, *sl 1, k2; rep from * to end—45 sts. **Rnd 8** With A, knit. Rep rnds 5–8 three times more, then rnds 5–6 once—51 sts (12 sts between thumb gusset markers). **Next rnd** With A, sl 1, drop marker, place next 12 sts on scrap yarn for thumb, drop marker, cast on 3 sts, k2, *sl 1, k2; rep from * to end—42 sts. **Next rnd** With A, knit.

HAND
Beg with rnd 1, cont in slip st pat until piece measures 6½"/16.5cm from last rnd of cuff, end with rnd 2.

TOP SHAPING
Dec rnd 1 With A, *[sl 1, ssk, sl 1, k2] twice, sl 1, k2tog, sl 1, k2, sl 1, k2tog; rep from * once more—34 sts. With A, knit next rnd. **Dec rnd 2** With B,*[k1, sl 1, ssk, sl 1] twice, k1, sl 1, k2tog, sl 1, k1, sl 1; rep from * once more—28 sts. With B, knit next rnd. **Dec rnd 3** With A, *[ssk] twice, k6, [k2tog] twice; rep from * once more—20 sts. With A, knit next rnd. With A, graft sts tog using Kitchener st or 3-needle bind-off.

THUMB
Place 12 thumb gusset sts over 2 larger needles. **Next rnd** Join A and knit across sts, then pick up and k 3 st over cast-on of thumb opening—15 sts. Divide sts evenly over 3 needles. Join and pm for beg of rnds. **Next rnd** With A, knit. Drop A. Cont in St st as foll: **Rnds 1 and 2** With B, knit. **Rnds 3 and 4** With A, knit. Rep rnds 1–4 for 2"/5cm.

TOP SHAPING
Keeping to color pat as established, work as foll: **Dec rnd 1** [K1, k2tog] 5 times—10 sts. Knit next rnd. **Dec rnd 2** [K2tog] 5 times—5 sts. Cut yarn leaving a 6"/15cm tail and thread through rem sts. Pull tog tightly and secure end. ■

Gauge
23 sts and 28 rnds to 4"/10cm over slip st pat using larger dpns. *Take time to check gauge.*

Ribbed Fingerless Mitts

Deceptively simple looking, these mitts are packed with interesting techniques, including diagonal and asymmetrical ribs. Contrasting edgings add more visual interest.

DESIGNED BY FAINA GOBERSTEIN

Size
Instructions are written for one size.

Knitted Measurements
Hand circumference 8"/20.5cm
Length approx 8¼"/21cm

Materials
■ 1 1¾oz/50g hank (each approx 164yd/150m) of *Cascade 220 Sport* (Peruvian highland wool) each in #8012 doeskin heather (MC) and #8013 walnut heather (CC)

■ One set (5) size 4 (3.5mm) double-pointed needles (dpns) *or size to obtain gauge*

■ Stitch markers

Stitch Glossary
2-st LT With RH needle behind LH needle, skip the first st and k 2nd st tbl, insert RH needle into backs of both sts, k2tog tbl.

Diagonal Rib
(multiple of 3 sts)
Rnd 1 *Sl 1 wyib, p2; rep from * around.
Rnd 2 *2-st LT, p1; rep from * around
Rnd 3 P1, *sl 1 wyib, p2; rep from * around to last 2 sts, end sl 1 wyib, p1.
Rnd 4 *P1, 2-st LT; rep from * around.
Rnd 5 *P2, sl 1 wyib; rep from * around to last 3 sts, end p2, sl next st to RH needle, remove marker, sl st back to LH needle, pm.
Rnd 6 *2-st LT, p1; rep from * to end, sl next st to RH needle, remove marker, sl st back to LH needle, pm, p1.
Rep rnds 1–6 for diagonal rib.

Asymmetrical V Rib
(multiple of 6 sts)
Rnds 1–3 *K4, p2; rep from * around.
Rnd 4 *K1, working between st on RH needle and next st on LH needle, insert RH needle under next 2 strands and draw up a long loop, leave loop on RH needle, k2, draw up a 2nd long loop in same space and leave on RH needle, k1, p2; rep from * around.

Rnd 5 *K1, sl long loop wyib, k2, sl long loop wyib, k1, p2; rep from * around.
Rnd 6 *K2tog, k2, ssk, p2; rep from * around.
Rnd 7 Rep rnd 1.
Rep rnds 4–7 for asymmetrical V rib.

Left Glove
CUFF
With CC, cast on 54 sts. Divide sts over 4 needles. Join, taking care not to twist sts on needles, pm for beg of rnds.
Rnd 1 Purl.
Rnd 2 Knit.
Rnd 3 Purl.
Rnds 4–10 Work rnds 1–6 of diagonal rib once, then rnd 1 once.
Rnd 11 Purl.
Rnd 12 Knit.
Rnd 13 Purl.

HAND
Change to MC. Cont in asymmetrical V rib until piece measures 5¾"/14.5cm from beg, end with rnd 6.

THUMB PLACEMENT
Next rnd Work rnd 7 of asymmetrical V rib to last 9 sts, k6 onto waste yarn, sl these 6 sts back to LH needle; with working yarn k1, p2, k4, p2.

Gauge
27 sts and 34 rnds to 4"/10cm over asymmetrical V rib using size 4 (3.5mm) dpns. *Take time to check gauge.*

Ribbed Fingerless Mitts 30

Next rnd *K1, working between st on RH needle and next st on LH needle, insert RH needle under next 2 strands and draw up a long loop, leave loop on RH needle, k2, draw up a 2nd long loop in same space and leave on RH needle, k1, p2; rep from * around to last 6 sts, end k4, p2.

Next rnd *K1, sl long loop wyib, k2, sl long loop wyib, k1, p2; rep from * around to last 6 sts, end k4, p2.

Next rnd *K2tog, k2, ssk, p2; rep from * to last 6 sts, k4, p2.

Next rnd *K4, p2; rep from * around. Beg with rnd 4, cont in asymmetrical V rib until piece measures 7"/18cm from beg, end with rnd 6. Change to CC. Rep rnds 1–12 of cuff. Bind off purlwise.

THUMB
Remove waste yarn and place 12 live sts on dpns as foll: 6 sts below thumb opening on needle 2 and 6 sts above opening on needle 4. Join yarn to the right of needle 2; with needle 1 pick up and k 3 sts along side edge of opening; k 6 sts on needle 2; with needle 3 pick up and k 2 sts along side edge of opening; k 6 sts on needle 4—17 sts. Divide sts evenly between 4 needles. Join and pm for beg of rnds.
Rnds 1–10 Knit.
Rnd 11 Purl.
Rnd 12 Knit.
Rnd 13 Purl. Bind off purlwise.

Right Glove
Work same as left glove to thumb placement.

THUMB PLACEMENT
Next rnd Work rnd 7 of asymmetrical V rib over first 30 sts, k6 onto waste yarn, sl these 6 sts back to LH needle; with working yarn, *k4, p2; rep from * to end.

Next rnd *K1, working between st on RH needle and next st on LH needle, insert RH needle under next 2 strands and draw up a long loop, leave loop on RH needle, k2, draw up a 2nd long loop in same space and leave on RH needle, k1, p2; rep from * to last 24 sts; k4, p2, **k1, working between st on RH needle and next st on LH needle, insert RH needle under next 2 strands and draw up a long loop, leave loop on RH needle, k2, draw up a 2nd long loop in same space and leave on RH needle, k1, p2; rep from ** to end.

Next rnd *K1, sl long loop wyib, k2, sl long loop wyib, k1, p2; rep from * around to last 24 sts; k4, p2, **k1, sl long loop wyib, k2, sl long loop wyib, k1, p2; rep from ** to end.

Next rnd *K2tog, k2, ssk, p2; rep from * to last 24 sts; k4, p2; **k2tog, k2, ssk, p2; rep from ** to end.

Next rnd *K4, p2; rep from * around. Beg with rnd 4, cont in asymmetrical V rib until piece measures 7"/18cm from beg, end with rnd 6. Change to CC. Rep rnds 1–12 of cuff. Bind off purlwise.

THUMB
Remove waste yarn and place 12 live sts on dpn as foll: 6 sts below thumb opening on needle 2 and 6 sts above opening on needle 4. Join yarn to the right of needle 2; with needle 1 pick up and k 2 sts along side edge of opening; k 6 sts on needle 2; with needle 3 pick up and k 3 sts along side edge of opening; k 6 sts on needle 4—17 sts. Divide sts evenly between 4 needles. Join and pm for beg of rnds.
Rnds 1–10 Knit.
Rnd 11 Purl.
Rnd 12 Knit.
Rnd 13 Purl. Bind off purlwise. ■

31

Embroidered Mushroom Cap

Bring your favorite woodland fairy tales from childhood back to life with this unique wood grain–inspired hat topped off with embroidery.

DESIGNED BY PAT OLSKI

Size
Instructions are written for one size.

Knitted Measurements
Head circumference 19"/48cm
Depth 7¾"/19.5cm

Materials
■ 1 1¾oz/50g hank (each approx 164yd/150m) of *Cascade 220 Sport* (Peruvian highland wool) each in #4002 jet (A), #8401 silver grey (B), #9404 ruby (C) and #8010 natural (D)

■ Sizes 3 and 4 (3.25 and 3.5mm) circular needles, 16"/40cm long *or size to obtain gauge*

■ One set (5) size 4 (3.5mm) double-pointed needles (dpns)

■ Stitch markers

Note
To work in the rnd, always read chart from right to left.

Hat
With smaller circular needle and C, cast on 124 sts. Join and pm taking care not to twist sts on needle. Work in k1, p1 rib for 8 rnds. Change to larger needle and A.
Next rnd [K31, pm] 3 times, k31. Cont in St st (knit every rnd) as foll:
BEG CHART PAT
Rnd 1 Work 31-st rep 4 times. Cont to foll chart in this way to rnd 26.

CROWN SHAPING
Change to dpns (dividing sts evenly between 4 needles) when there are too few sts on circular needle.
Rnd 27 Work 31-st rep 4 times. Cont to foll chart in this way to rnd 48, working each k2tog dec in color shown on chart—16 sts. Cut yarns leaving 8"/20.5cm tails and thread through rem sts. Pull tog tightly and secure ends.

Finishing
EMBROIDERY
For each mushroom, embroider stem with vertical rows of chain stitches; use C for small mushroom and D for medium and large mushrooms. For underside of mushroom cap, embroider horizontal rows of chain stitches using D. For mushroom caps, embroider horizontal rows of chain stitches following the contour of the cap using C. For small and large mushrooms, accent caps with French knots using D (see page 94). ■

Gauge
26 sts and 30 rnds to 4"/10cm over St st and chart pat using larger circular needle.
Take time to check gauge.

Embroidered Mushroom Cap

31

Color Key

- ▢ Jet (A)
- ☐ Silver Grey (B)

Stitch Key

- ☐ Knit
- ◩ K2tog using A
- ◰ K2tog using B
- ▢ No stitch

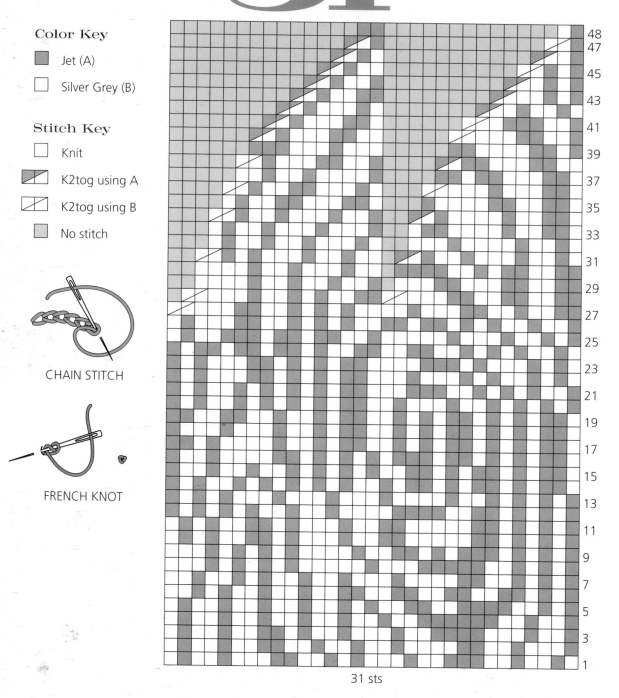

CHAIN STITCH

FRENCH KNOT

31 sts

Zigzag Lace Scarf

Lean to the left, now a little to the right… With an easy-to-remember pattern, this modern take on lace is the perfect project to take on the go.

DESIGNED BY LOIS S. YOUNG

Size
Instructions are written for one size.

Knitted Measurements
6½" x 59"/16.5cm x 150cm

Materials
■ 2 1¾oz/50g hanks (each approx 164yd/150m) of *Cascade 220 Sport* (Peruvian highland wool) in #9325 westpoint blue heather

■ One pair size 8 (5mm) needles *or size to obtain gauge*

Scarf
Cast on 29 sts. Knit next 6 rows. Cont in leaning lace pat as foll:
RS rows 1–19 K3, [(ssk, yo) 3 times, k2] twice, [ssk, yo] 3 times, k4.
Row 2 and all WS rows Knit.
RS rows 21–39 K4, [(yo, k2tog) 3 times, k2] twice, [yo, k2tog] 3 times, k3.
Row 40 Knit. Rep rows 1–40 ten times more, then work rows 1–20 once. Piece

should measure approx 58½"/148.5cm from beg. Knit next 5 rows. Bind off loosely knitwise.

Finishing
Block piece lightly to measurements. ■

Gauge
29 sts to 6½"/16.5cm and 40 rows to 5"/12.5cm over leaning lace pat using size 8 (5mm) needles (after blocking). *Take time to check gauge.*

Petal-Motif Scarf

Channel some flower power when you don this delightful Fair Isle scarf. It's worked in two pieces and grafted together, then tipped with fringe.

DESIGNED BY DIANE ZANGL

Size
Instructions are written for one size.

Knitted Measurements
Length 60"/152.5cm (without fringe)
Width 7"/17.5cm

Materials
- 7 1¾ oz/50g hanks (each approx 164yd/150m) of *Cascade 220 Sport* (Peruvian highland wool) in #9421 blue hawaii (MC)
- 1 hank each #8010 natural (A) and #8400 charcoal grey (B), and #4002 jet (C)
- One each size 4 and 5 (3.5 and 3.75 mm) circular needles, 16"/40cm long *or size to obtain gauge*
- Crochet hook for provisional cast on and attaching fringe
- Scrap yarn

Note
When working color pat, carry yarns loosely across back of work to avoid puckering.

Scarf
FIRST HALF
With crochet hook and scrap yarn, chain 86 sts. With smaller needle and MC, pick up one st through back of each of 84 ch sts. Place marker and join, being careful not to twist sts. Work in St st (k every rnd) until piece measures 23"/58.5cm from beg. Change to larger needles.

BEG CHART
Next rnd Work rnd 1 of chart, working 14-st rep 6 times around.
Cont to work chart pat until 28 rnds are complete, then rep rnds 1–6 once more. Change to smaller needles and cont in MC only. Work 10 rnds. Bind off.

SECOND HALF
Carefully remove scrap yarn chain and place open sts on smaller needle—84 sts. Attach MC and work same as for first half.

Finishing
Add fringe as foll: Cut 90 strands of yarn, each 12"/30.5cm long. Holding 3 strands tog, fold in half, insert crochet hook through both layers in one bound-off edge, pull fold of fringe through stitches. Pull ends through loop, fastening off tightly. Add one 3-strand fringe through every 3rd stitch of each bound-off edge. Trim fringe evenly. ■

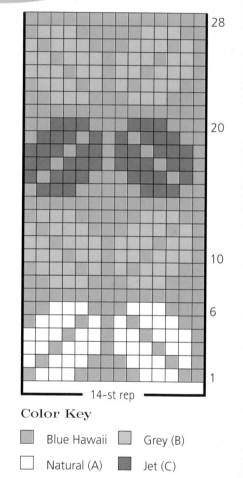

14-st rep

Color Key
- Blue Hawaii
- Grey (B)
- Natural (A)
- Jet (C)

Gauges
24 sts and 32 rnds to 4"/10cm over St st using smaller needles.
24 sts and 24 rnds to 4"10cm over chart pat using larger needles. *Take time to check gauges.*

Hourglass Mitts

This echoing cable pattern is sure to become a favorite. With cabling done only on the right side, a simple stockinette back and thumb gusset, this unisex design is timeless.

DESIGNED BY ANASTASIA BLAES

Size
Instructions are written for one size.

Knitted Measurements
Hand circumference 6½"/16.5cm (unstretched)
Length approx 7¼"/18.5cm

Materials
- 2 1¾oz/50g hanks (each approx 164yd/150m) of *Cascade 220 Sport* (Peruvian highland wool) in #8903 primaverra
- One set (4) size 3 (3.25mm) ouble-pointed needles (dpns) *or size to obtain gauge*
- Cable needle (cn)
- Stitch markers

Note
To work in the rnd, always read chart from right to left.

Stitch Glossary
2-st RC Sl next st to cn and hold to *back*, k1, k1 from cn.
2-st LC Sl next st to cn and to *front*, k1, k1, from cn.
2-st RPC Sl next st to cn and hold to *back*, k1, p1, from cn.
2-st LPC Sl next st to cn and hold to *front*, p1, k1, from cn.
3-st RPC Sl next 2 sts to cn and hold to *back*, k1, p2 from cn.
3-st LPC Sl next st to cn and hold to *front*, p2, k1 from cn.

Left Mitt
Cast on 55 sts. Divide sts over 3 needles. Join, taking care not to twist sts on needles, pm for beg of rnds.

EDGING
Rnds 1–5 Purl.
Rnd 6 K, inc 7 sts evenly spaced around—62 sts.
SET-UP RNDS
Rnds 1–8 [K1, p1] 7 times, k1, [k1, p4] 6 times, k1, [k1, p1] 8 times.
BEG CHART PAT

Rnd 1 [K1, p1] 7 times, k1, work chart over next 31 sts, k1, [k1, p1] 8 times. Keeping sts each side of chart in rib pat as established, cont to foll chart in this way through rnd 16.

THUMB GUSSET
Rnd 17 [K1, p1] 4 times, k1, pm, M1, [p1, k1] twice, pm, p1, k1, work chart over next 31 sts, [k1, p1] 8 times—63 sts (5 sts between thumb gusset markers).
Rnd 18 [K1, p1] 4 times, k1, sl marker, k1, [p1, k1] to next marker, sl marker, p1, k1, work chart over next 31 sts, [k1, p1] 8 times.
Rnd 19 [K1, p1] 4 times, k1, sl marker, M1, k1, [p1, k1] to next marker, sl marker, p1, k1, work chart over next 31 sts, [k1, p1] 8 times—64 sts.
Rnd 20 [K1, p1] 4 times, k1, sl marker, [p1, k1] to next marker, sl marker, p1, k1, work chart over next 31 sts, [k1, p1] 8 times.
Rnd 21 [K1, p1] 4 times, k1, sl marker, M1, [p1, k1] to next marker, sl marker, p1, k1, work chart over next 31 sts, [k1, p1] 8 times—65 sts.
Rnd 22 [K1, p1] 4 times, k1, sl marker, k1, [p1, k1] to next marker, sl marker, p1, k1, work chart over next 31 sts, [k1, p1] 8 times.

Gauge
26 sts and 36 rnds to 4"/10cm over St st using size 3 (3.25mm) dpns. *Take time to check gauge.*

Hourglass Mitts

Quick Tip
With two and three stitch cables, practice cabling without a cable needle to save yourself time.

Rnd 23 [K1, p1] 4 times, k1, sl marker, M1, k1, [p1, k1] to next marker, sl marker, p1, k1, work chart over next 31 sts, [k1, p1] 8 times—66 sts.
Rnd 24 [K1, p1] 4 times, k1, sl marker, [p1, k1] to next marker, sl marker, p1, k1, work chart over next 31 sts, [k1, p1] 8 times.
Rnds 25–28 Rep rnds 21–24—68 sts.
Rnds 29–32 Rep rnds 21–24—70 sts.
Rnds 33–36 Rep rnds 21–24—72 sts.

Rnds 37–39 Rep rnds 21–24—74 sts.
Rnd 40 [K1, p1] 4 times, k1, drop marker, place next 16 sts on scrap yarn, drop marker, cast on 4 sts over thumb opening, p1, k1, work chart over next 31 sts, [k1, p1] 8 times—62 sts. Keeping sts each side of chart in rib pat as established, cont to foll chart in this way through rnd 60.
Next 8 rnds [K1, p1] 7 times, k1, [k1, p4] 6 times, k1, [k1, p1] 8 times.

EDGING
Rnd 1 Knit, dec 7 sts evenly spaced around—55 sts.
Rnds 2–4 Purl. Bind off purlwise.

THUMB
Place 16 thumb gusset sts over 2 needles.
Next rnd Join yarn and work [p1, k1] 8 times over first 2 needles; with 3rd needle, pick up and k 4 sts in cast-on sts of thumb opening, pm for beg of rnds—20 sts. Divide sts evenly over 3 needles. Work around in p1, k1 rib for 9 rnds more. P next 2 rnds. Bind off purlwise.

Right Mitt
Work same as left fingerless glove to thumb gusset.

THUMB GUSSET
Rnd 17 [K1, p1] 7 times, k1, work chart over next 31 sts, k1, p1, pm, [k1, p1] twice, M1, pm, [k1, p1] 5 times—63 sts (5 sts between thumb gusset markers).
Rnd 18 [K1, p1] 7 times, k1, work chart over next 31 sts, k1, p1, sl marker, [k1, p1] twice, k1, sl marker, [k1, p1] 5 times.
Rnd 19 [K1, p1] 7 times, k1, work chart over next 31 sts, k1, p1, sl marker, [k1, p1] twice, k1, M1, sl marker, [k1, p1] 5 times—64 sts.
Rnd 20 [K1, p1] 7 times, k1, work chart over next 31 sts, k1, p1, sl marker, [k1, p1] to next marker, sl marker, [k1, p1] 5 times.
Rnd 21 [K1, p1] 7 times, k1, work chart over next 31 sts, k1, p1, sl marker, [k1, p1] to next marker, M1, sl marker, [k1, p1] 5 times—65 sts.
Rnd 22 [K1, p1] 7 times, k1, work chart over next 31 sts, k1, p1, sl marker, [k1,

p1] to 1 st before next marker, k1, sl
marker, [k1, p1] 5 times.

Rnd 23 [K1, p1] 7 times, k1, work chart
over next 31 sts, k1, p1, sl marker, [k1,
p1] to 1 st before next marker, k1, M1, sl
marker, [k1, p1] 5 times—66 sts.

Rnd 24 [K1, p1] 7 times, k1, work chart
over next 31 sts, k1, p1, sl marker,
[k1, p1] to next marker, sl marker, [k1,
p1] 5 times. Slipping markers every rnd,
cont as foll:

Rnds 25–28 Rep rnds 21-24—68 sts.

Rnds 29–32 Rep rnds 21-24—70 sts.

Rnds 33–36 Rep rnds 21-24—72 sts.

Rnds 37–39 Rep rnds 21-24—74 sts.

Rnd 40 [K1, p1] 7 times, k1, drop marker,
work chart over next 31 sts, k1, p1, drop
marker, place next 16 sts on scrap yarn,
drop marker, cast on 4 sts over thumb
opening, [k1, p1] 5 times—62 sts.
Keeping sts each side of chart in rib pat
as established, cont to foll chart in this
way through rnd 60. Cont to work same
as left fingerless glove.

Finishing
Sew gap between thumb and hand
closed. Block pieces to measurements. ∎

Stitch Key

□	Knit	⊠	2-st RPC
−	Purl	⊠	2-st LPC
⋏	S2KP	⊠	3-st RPC
⊠	2-st RC	⊠	3-st LPC
⊠	2-st LC	▨	No stitch

31 sts

Double-Knit Checkerboard Scarf

To get this graphic patterning the front and back of the fabric are worked at the same time, resulting in an extra-thick scarf. Wonderful for the knitter looking for the next challenge!

DESIGNED BY LILY M. CHIN

Size
Instructions are written for one size.

Knitted Measurements
Approx 6¼" x 68"/16cm x 173cm

Materials
- 2 1¾ oz/50g hanks (each approx 164yd/150m) of *Cascade 220 Sport* (Peruvian highland wool) each in #9459 yakima heather (A) and #4010 straw (B)
- Contrasting sport-weight cotton (waste yarn)
- One pair size 6 (4mm) needles *or size to obtain gauge*
- Size E/4 (3.5mm) crochet hook (for chain-st provisional cast-on)

Notes
1) All odd rows are side 1 and all even rows are side 2.
2) Twist colors at beg of every row to prevent holes.

Scarf
With crochet hook and waste yarn, ch 33 for chain-st provisional cast-on. Cut yarn and draw end though lp on hook. Turn ch so bottom lps are at top and cut end is at left. With A, beg 2 lps from right end, *pick up and k 1 st in next lp, yo; rep from * 26 times more, then pick up and k 1 st each of next 2 lps—56 sts.

CHECKERBOARD PAT
Row 1 (side 1) With A, k2tog, bring both yarns to front, p1 with B, [bring both yarns to back, k1 with A, bring both yarns to front, p1 with B] twice, *[bring both yarns to back, k1 with B, bring both yarns to front, p1 with A] 3 times, [bring both yarns to back, k1 with A, bring both yarns to front, p1 with B] 3 times; rep from *, ending last rep with, p2tog with B—54 sts (27 sts on each side).
Row 2 (side 2) *[Bring both yarns to back, k1 with B, bring both yarns to front, p1 with A] 3 times**, [bring both yarns to back, k1 with A, bring both yarns to front, p1 with B] 3 times; rep from *, end last rep at **.
Row 3 (side 1) *[Bring both yarns to back, k1 with A, bring both yarns to front, p1 with B] 3 times**, [bring both yarns to back, k1 with B, bring both

yarns to front, p1 with A] 3 times; rep from *, end last rep at **.
Row 4 (side 2) Rep row 2.
Rows 5 and 7 Rep row 2.
Rows 6 and 8 Rep row 3.
Rows 9 and 11 Rep row 3.
Rows 10 and 12 Rep row 2.
Rows 13–20 Rep rows 5–12.

STRIPE PAT
Odd rows 21–39 Rep row 2.
Even rows 22–40 Rep row 3.
Row 41 Rep row 3. Rep rows 2–41 until piece measures approx 68"/173cm from beg, end with row 20. Leave sts on needle.

Finishing
To finish top edge, place all A sts on one needle and all B sts on a 2nd needle. With either A or B, graft top edge tog using Kitchener st. To finish bottom edge, release cut end from lp of waste yarn ch. Pulling out 1 ch at a time, place all A sts on one needle and all B sts on a 2nd needle. With either A or B, graft bottom edge tog using Kitchener st. Block piece to measurements. ■

Gauge
17 sts and 22 rows to 4"/10cm over double-knit chart pat using size 6 (4mm) needles. *Take time to check gauge.*

Cabled Block Scarf

Coming together like an optical illusion, this scarf comprises cabled blocks knit on the bias, turned and seamed together. It's as intriguing as it is enjoyable to knit.

DESIGNED BY LOIS S. YOUNG

Size
Instructions are written for one size.

Knitted Measurements
Length 68"/172.5cm
Width 9.5"/24cm

Materials
- 5 1¾ oz/50g hanks (each approx 164yd/150m) of *Cascade 220 Sport* (Peruvian highland wool) in #8021 beige
- Size 5 (3.75 mm) circular needle, 22"/56cm *or size to obtain gauge*
- Cable needle (cn)

Note
Scarf consists of 7 blocks. Each block is made from 4 diagonals, which are worked separately and joined once 4 diagonals have been completed. When all 7 blocks have been joined, piece is trimmed with garter stitch borders, which are picked up and knit along all 4 edges.

Stitch Glossary
M1 (looped make 1)
Make 1 st by casting on 1 st using backward-loop method.
6-st LC Sl 3 sts to cn, hold to *front*, k3, k3 from cn.
2-st LC Sl 1 st to cn, hold to *front*, k1, k1 from cn.
4-st LC Sl 2 sts to cn, hold to *front*, k2, k2 from cn.

2-st RC Sl 1 st to cn, hold to *back*, k1, k1 from cn.
4-st RC Sl 2 sts to cn, hold to *back*, k2, k2 from cn.

Block (make 7)
Cast on 4 sts. **Next row (WS)** Purl.

BEG CHART
Work foll chart until 63 rows are complete. Cut yarn leaving 8"/20.5cm tail. Place rem 4 sts on holder. Rep for 3 diagonals more. When 4 diagonals have been worked, with tapestry needle, thread tail of last diagonal worked through open sts of all 4 diagonals and secure. Sew seams using whip st.

Finishing
Sew completed blocks tog in one long strip using whip st.

BORDERS
With RS facing, pick up and k 53 sts along one short edge. Knit 6 rows. Bind off. Rep for opposite short edge. With RS facing, beg at garter st border, pick up and k 387 sts evenly along one long side edge. Knit 6 rows. Bind off. Rep for opposite long side. Block lightly. ■

Gauge
Each 36-st, 64-row square has 4.25"/11cm sides in pat st after blocking. *Take time to check gauge.*

36
Cabled Block Scarf

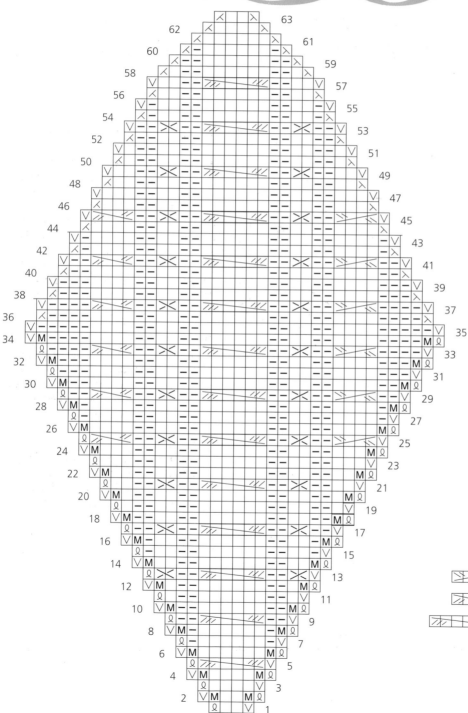

Stitch Key

☐	K on RS, p on WS
─	P on RS, k on WS
℧	Kl tbl
╱	K2tog on RS, p2tog on WS
╲	K2tog tbl on RS, p2tog tbl on WS
∨	Sl 1 pwise wyif
M	M1
⧄	2-st RC
⧅	2-st LC
⧄⧄	4-st RC
⧅⧅	4-st LC
⧄⧄⧄	6-st LC

Flower-Motif Beanie

With intricate cabling and a twisted-stitch ribbed brim, this richly textured cap will take your cabling skills to the next level.

DESIGNED BY LIDIA KARABINECH

Size
Instructions are written for one size.

Knitted Measurements
Circumference 19"/48cm at ribbing, 22"/56cm at widest part
Depth 8.5"/21.5cm

Materials
■ 1 1¾oz/50g hank (each approx 164yd/150m) of *Cascade 220 Sport* (Peruvian highland wool) in #8895 Christmas red

■ One each size 2 and 5 (2.75 and 3.75mm) circular needles, 16"/40 cm long *or size to obtain gauge*

■ One set size 5 (3.75mm) double-pointed needles (dpns)

■ Cable needle (cn)

■ Stitch markers

Stitch Glossary
K2tog Sl 1 from back twice, place 2 sts back to LH, k 2 sts tog.
K2tog tbl Knit 2 sts tog through the back loops.
K1 tbl K into *back* of st.
2-st RT Sl 1 to cn and hold to *back*, k1 tbl, k1 tbl from cn.
2-st LT Sl 1 to cn and hold to *front*, k1 tbl, k1 tbl from cn.
2-st RPT Sl 1 to cn and hold to *back*, k1 tbl, p1 from cn.
2-st LPT Sl 1 to cn and hold to *front*, p1, k1 tbl from cn.

3-st RPT Sl 1 to cn and hold to *back*, k2 tbl, p1 from cn.
3-st LPT Sl 1 to cn and hold to *front*, k2 tbl, p1 from cn. With smaller circular needle, cast on 120 sts. Join and pm, taking care not to twist sts.
Rnds 1–10 *K tbl, p1; rep from * to end of rnd. Change to larger circular needle.
Next (inc) rnd *M1 p-st, K1, M1 p-st, P2, M1 p-st, P1, K1, M1 p-st, P1, K1, P5, K1, P1, M1 p-st, K1, P5, K1, M1 p-st, P1, K1, P5, K1, P1; rep from * 3 times more—144 sts.

BEG CHART
Next rnd Work rnd 1 of chart, working 18-st rep 8 times around. Cont to work chart in this manner through rnd 24. Rep rnds 1–16 once more. Piece measures approx 6"/15cm from beg.

SHAPE CROWN
Note Change to dpns when sts no longer fit comfortably on circular needle.
Rnd 1 (dec) *P1, K2tog tbl, p3, k6 tbl, p3, k2tog (see stitch glossary), p1; rep from * to end—128 sts.
Rnd 2 *2-st RPT, p3, k6 tbl, p3, 2-st LPT; rep from * to end.

Gauge
25 sts and 30 rnds to 4"/10cm over pat st using larger needle. *Take time to check gauge.*

Flower-Motif Beanie

Rnd 3 Remove marker, k1 tbl, pm, *p4, k6 tbl, p4, 2-st RT; rep from * to end.

Rnd 4 Remove marker, p1, pm, *p3, k6 tbl, p3, 2-st RPT, 2-st LPT; rep from * to end.

Rnd 5 (dec) *P2, k2tog, k4 tbl, k2tog tbl, p2, k1 tbl, p2, k1 tbl; rep from * to end—112 sts.

Rnd 6 *P1, 3-st RPT , 2-st RT, 3-st LPT, p1, k1 tbl, p2, k1 tb1; rep from * to end.

Rnd 7 *P1, 2-st RPT, p1, k2 tbl, p1, 2-st LPT, p1, k1 tbl, p2, k1 tbl; rep from * to end.

Rnd 8 (dec) *2-st RPT, p1, 2-st RPT, 2-st LPT, P1, 2-st LPT, k2tog tbl, k2tog; rep from * to end—96 sts.

Rnd 9 *P3, k1 tbl, p2, k1tbl, p3, 2-st RT ; rep from * to end.

Rnd 10 (dec) Remove marker, p1, pm, *p2, k2tog tbl, k2tog, p2, 2-st RPT, 2-st LPT; rep from * to end—80 sts.

Rnd 11 (dec) *P2, k2tog, p2, k1 tbl, p2, k1 tbl; rep from * to end—72 sts.

Rnd 12 (dec) Remove m, p1, pm, *p1, k1 tbl, p1, k2tog, p2, k2tog tbl, rep from * to end—56 sts.

Rnd 13 (dec) *P1, k1 tbl, p1, k2tog tbl, k2tog; rep from * to end—40 sts.

Rnd 14 (dec) *P1, k1 tbl, p1, k2tog, rep from * to end—32 sts.

Rnd 15 (dec) *K2tog; rep from * to end—16 sts.

Rnd 16 (dec) K2tog tbl; rep from * to end—8 sts.

Finishing

Cut yarn, leaving a generous tail. Draw tail through rem sts on needle. Pull gently to close hole. ∎

18-st rep

Stitch Key

Q	K1 tbl
—	Purl
⧄	2-st RT
⧄	2-st LT
⧄	2-st RPT
⧄	2-st LPT
⧄	3-st RPT
⧄	3-st LPT

Tulip Mittens

These Fair Isle tulip mittens are worked in a traditional Norwegian-style with thumb gusset and slip-stitch ribbed cuffs. Wear these beauties while walking in the garden, dreaming of spring.

DESIGNED BY BARB BROWN

Size
Instructions are written for one size.

Knitted Measurements
Hand circumference 7½"/19cm
Length of cuff Approx 2¾"/7cm

Materials
■ 1 1¾oz/50g hank (each approx 164yd/150m) of *Cascade 220 Sport* (Peruvian highland wool) each in #7804 shrimp (MC) and #9408 cordovan (CC)
■ One set (4) size 3 (3.25mm) double-pointed needles (dpns) *or size to obtain gauge*
■ Stitch markers

Note
To work in the rnd, always read charts from right to left.

Stitch Glossary
M1R (make 1 right) Insert left needle from *back* to *front* into the horizontal strand between the last st worked and the next st on left needle. Using color indicated on chart, k this strand through the front lp to twist the st.
M1L (make 1 left) Insert left needle from *front* to *back* into the horizontal strand between the last st worked and the next st on left needle. Using color indicated on chart, k this strand tbl to twist the st.

Right Mitten
CUFF
With CC, cast on 54 sts. Divide sts over 4 needles. Join taking care not to twist sts on needles, pm for beg of rnds.
Next rnd *K1, p1; rep from * around. Cont in sl st rib as foll:
Rnd 1 With MC, *sl 1 wyib, k1; rep from * around.
Rnd 2 With CC, k. Rep these 2 rnds until piece measures 2¾"/7cm from beg, end with rnd 2.

BEG CHART PAT I
Beg chart on rnd 1 and work even through rnd 5.

THUMB GUSSET
Rnd 6 Work first 4 sts of chart, pm, with MC: M1L, k next st (st 5 on chart), M1R, pm, work to end of rnd—56 sts.

BEG CHART PAT II
Rnd 7 Work first 4 sts of chart I, sl marker, beg chart II on rnd 2 and work next 3 sts, sl marker, work to end of chart I. Cont to foll charts in this way through rnd 32 of chart I and rnd 27 of chart II—72 sts.
Rnd 33 Work first 4 sts of chart I, place 19 thumb sts on scrap yarn, with MC, cast on 1 st over thumb opening, work to end of rnd—54 sts. Cont to work to top of chart I, dec top of mitten as shown—26 sts. Using CC, weave sts tog using Kitchener st or 3-needle bind-off.

THUMB
Place 19 sts on scrap yarn on 2 dpns (9 sts on first needle and 10 sts on 2nd needle). With 3rd needle and CC, pick up and k 1 st in cast-on st of thumb opening; cont to work as foll: *k1 with MC, k1 with CC; rep from * around 8 times more, end k1 with MC, pm for beg of rnds—20 sts. Divide sts evenly over 4 needles (5 sts on each). Cont in stripe pat as foll:
Rnd 1 *K1 with CC, k1 with MC; rep from * around. Rep this rnd 12 times more. Cut MC. Cont with CC only as foll:

Gauge
29 sts and 30 rnds to 4"/10cm over chart pats using size 3 (3.25mm) dpns. *Take time to check gauge.*

38 Tulip Mittens

CHART II

19 sts

Color Key

■ Shrimp (MC)

■ Cordovan (CC)

Symbol Key

 Right thumb placement

✱ Left thumb placement

Stitch Key

☐ Knit

⧄ K2tog

⧅ Ssk

M1R

M1L

■ No Stitch

TOP SHAPING

Dec rnd 1 [K2, k2tog] 5 times—15 sts.
Dec rnd 2 [K1, k2tog] 5 times—10 sts.
Dec rnd 3 [K2tog] 5 times—5 sts.
Cut yarn leaving a 6"/15cm tail. Thread tail in tapestry needle, then thread through rem sts. Pull tog tightly and secure end. Weave in MC.

Left Mitten

Work same as right mitten to thumb gusset.

THUMB GUSSET

Rnd 6 Work first 22 sts of chart, pm, with MC: M1L, k next st (st 23 on chart), M1R, pm, work to end of rnd—56 sts.

BEG CHART PAT II

Rnd 7 Work first 22 sts of chart I, sl marker, beg chart II on rnd 2 and work next 3 sts, sl marker, work to end of chart I. Cont to foll charts in this way through rnd 32 of chart I and rnd 27 of chart II—72 sts.
Rnd 33 Work first 22 sts of chart I, place 19 thumb sts on scrap yarn, with MC, cast on 1 st over thumb opening, work to end of rnd—54 sts. Cont to work to top of chart I, dec top of mitten as shown—26 sts. Using CC, weave sts tog using Kitchener st or 3-needle bind-off. Cont to work same as right mitten.

Finishing

Sew gap between thumb and hand closed. Block pieces to measurements. ■

CHART I

Two-Color Cabled Mitts

Featuring a modern twist on a classic cable, these braided fingerless mitts are knit flat, joined in the round for the thumb and seamed up the side.

DESIGNED BY ANGELA JUERGEN

Size

Instructions are written for one size.

Knitted Measurements

Hand circumference 6"/15cm (unstretched)

Length approx 8"/20.5cm

Materials

■ 1 1¾oz/50g hank (each approx 164yd/150m) of *Cascade 220 Sport* (Peruvian highland wool) each in #7802 cerise (A) and #7822 vandyke brown (B)

■ One pair each sizes 4 and 6 (3.5 and 4mm) needles *or size to obtain gauge*

■ One set (4) size 6 (4mm) double-pointed needles (dpns)

■ Cable needle (cn)

■ Stitch markers

Notes

1) Mitts are worked back and forth on two needles.

2) Thumbs are worked in the rnd on dpns.

3) Do not carry colors across. Use a separate strand of color for each color section.

Rib Pattern

(multiple of 6 sts plus 2)

Row 1 (RS) K1, *p3, k3; rep from *, end k1.

Row 2 P1, *p3, k3; rep from *, end p1. Rep rows 1 and 2 for rib pat.

Right Mitt

With smaller needles and B, cast on 44 sts.

Rows 1–8 Rep rows 1 and 2 of rib pat 4 times. Change to larger needles. Cont in two-color cable pat as foll:

Row 9 (RS) With A: k5, p2, k6. With B: k6. With A: k6. With B: p2, k17.

Row 10 Keeping to color pat as established, k the knit sts and p the purl sts.

Rows 11–16 Rep rows 9 and 10 three times.

Row 17 With A: k5, p2, sl next 6 sts on cn and hold to *back.* With B: k6. With A: k6 from cn, then k6. With B: p2, k17.

Rows 18–24 Rep row 10.

Row 25 With A: k5, p2. With B: k6, sl next 6 sts on cn and hold to *front.* With A: k6, then k6 sts from cn. With B: p2, k17.

Rows 26–32 Rep row 10.

Row 33 With A: k5, p2, sl next 6 sts on cn and hold to *back.* With A: k next 6 sts. With B: k6 sts from cn. With A: k6. With B: p2, k17.

Rows 34–40 Rep row 10.

Row 41 With A: k5, p2, k6, sl next 6 sts on cn and hold to *front.* With A: k next 6 sts. With B: k6 sts from cn.

With B: p2, k 17.

Row 42 Rep row 10.

THUMB GUSSET

Row 43 (RS) Work 29 sts in pat as established, pm, M1, k2, M1, work to end—46 sts.

Row 44 Keeping to color pat as established, k the knit sts and p the purl sts, and sl markers.

Row 45 Work to marker, sl marker, M1, k4, M1, sl marker, work to end—48 sts.

Row 46 Rep row 44.

Row 47 Work to marker, sl marker, M1, k6, M1, sl marker, work to end—50 sts.

Row 48 Rep row 44.

Row 49 With A: k5, p2, sl next 6 sts on cn and hold to *back,* k next 6 sts, then k 6 sts from cn. With B: p2, k2, sl marker, M1, k8, M1, sl marker, work to end—52 sts.

Row 50 Rep row 44.

Row 51 Work to marker, sl marker, M1, k10, M1, sl marker, work to end—54 sts.

Row 52 Rep row 44.

Row 53 Work to marker, sl marker, M1, k12, M1, sl marker, work to end—56 sts.

Row 54 Rep row 44.

Row 55 Work to marker, drop marker, place 14 thumb sts on scrap yarn, drop marker, with B cast on 2 sts over thumb opening, work to end—44 sts.

Row 56 Keeping to color pat as established, k the knit sts and p the purl sts.

Row 57 With A: k5, p2, k6, sl next 6 sts

Gauge

22 sts and 34 rows to 4"/10cm over St st using larger needles. *Take time to check gauge.*

pick up and k 1 st each of next 2 cast-on sts of thumb opening, then 1 st after thumb opening, pm for beg of rnds—18 sts. Divide sts evenly over 3 needles (6 sts on each). Work around in St st (k every rnd) for 7 rnds.

Next (dec) rnd [K2tog, k7] twice—16 sts. Work around in k2, p2 rib for 8 rnds. Bind off in rib.

Left Mitt

Work same as right mitt to row 8. Change to larger needles. Cont in two-color cable pat as foll:

Row 9 (RS) With B: k17, p2. With A: k6. With B: k6. With A: k6, p2, k5.

Row 10 Keeping to color pat as established, k the knit sts and p the purl sts.

Rows 11–16 Rep rows 9 and 10 three times.

Row 17 With B: k17, p2. With A: k6, sl next 6 sts on cn and hold to *front*. With A: k next 6 sts. With B: k 6 sts from cn. With A: p2, k5.

Rows 18–24 Rep row 10.

Row 25 With B: k17, p2, sl next 6 sts on cn and hold to *back*. With A: k next 6 sts, then k 6 sts from cn. With B: k6. With A: p2, k5.

Rows 26–32 Rep row 10.

Row 33 With B: k17, p2. With A: k6, sl next 6 sts on cn and hold to *front*. With B: k next 6 sts. With A: k 6 sts from cn, p2, k5.

Rows 34–40 Rep row 10.

Row 41 With B: k17, p2, sl next 6 sts on cn and hold to back. With B: k next 6 sts. With A: k 6 sts from cn, k6, p2, k5.

Row 42 Rep row 10.

THUMB GUSSET

Row 43 (RS) Work 15 sts in pat as established, pm, M1, k2, M1, work to end—46 sts.

Row 44 Keeping to color pat as established, k the knit sts and p the purl sts, and sl markers.

Row 45 Work to marker, sl marker, M1, k4, M1, sl marker, k to end—48 sts.

Row 46 Rep row 44.

Row 47 Work to marker, sl marker, M1, k6, M1, sl marker, k to end—50 sts.

Row 48 Rep row 44.

Row 49 Work to marker, sl marker, M1, k8, M1, sl marker, k2, p2, k6, sl next 6 sts on cn and hold to *front*. With A, k next 6 sts, then k 6 sts from cn, p2, work to end—52 sts.

Row 50 Rep row 44.

Row 51 Work to marker, sl marker, M1, k10, M1, sl marker, work to end—54 sts.

Row 52 Rep row 44.

Row 53 Work to marker, sl marker, M1, k12, M1, sl marker, work to end—56 sts.

Row 54 Rep row 44.

Row 55 Work to marker, drop marker, place 14 thumb sts on scrap yarn, drop marker, with B, cast on 2 sts over thumb opening, k2, p2, work to end—44 sts.

Row 56 Keeping to color pat as established, k the knit sts and p the purl sts.

Row 57 With B: k17, p2, sl next 6 sts on cn and hold to *back*. With A: knit next 6 sts. With B: k 6 sts from cn. With A: k6, p2, k 5.

Rows 58–64 Rep row 56.

Row 65 With B: k17, p2. With A: k6, sl next 6 sts on cn and hold to *front*, k next 6 sts. With B: k 6 sts from cn. With A: p2, k5.

Rows 66 and 67 Rep row 56. Cut A. Change to smaller needles. Cont with B as foll:

Next row (WS) P5, k2, p18, k2, p17. Work in rib pat for 7 rows. Bind off in rib pat.

THUMB

Work same as right mitt.

Finishing

Sew gap between thumb and hand closed. Block pieces to measurements. ∎

---

on cn and hold to *front*. With B: k next 6 sts. With A: k 6 sts from cn. With B: p2, k17.

Rows 58–64 Rep row 56.

Row 65 With A: k5, p2, sl next 6 sts on cn and hold to *back*. With B: k next 6 sts. With A: k6 sts from cn, then k next 6 sts. With B: p2, k17.

Rows 66 and 67 Rep row 56. Cut A. Change to smaller needles. Cont with B as foll:

Next row (WS) P17, k2, p18, k2, p5. Work in rib pat for 7 rows. Bind off in rib pat.

THUMB

Place 14 sts on scrap yarn on 2 dpns (7 sts on first needle and 7 sts on 2nd needle). With 3rd needle, pick up and k 1 st before cast-on sts of thumb opening,

Drawstring Cowl/Hat

Everyone loves a two-for-one! As versatile as it is easy to knit, this cables, lace and ribs extravaganza can be worn around your neck as a cowl or on your head as a drawstring hat.

DESIGNED BY ANASTASIA BLAES

Size
Instructions are written for one size.

Knitted Measurements
Head circumference Approx 21.5"/54.5cm

Materials
- 1 1¾ oz/50g hank (each approx 164yd/150m) of *Cascade 220 Sport* (Peruvian highland wool) in #7809 violet
- Size 5 (3.75 mm) circular needle 16"/40cm
- Size 6 (4 mm) circular needle 16"/40cm *or size to obtain gauge*
- Stitch marker
- Cable needle (cn)

Stitch Glossary
C4F Sl 2 sts to cn and hold in front, k2, k2 from cn.
M1 (inc) Use LH needle to lift horizontal bar between st just worked and next st, k into back of lp.

Cowl/Hat
RIBBED CUFF
With size 5 (3.75mm) needle, cast on 108 sts. Pm and join, being careful not to twist.
Rnd 1 *P2, k1; rep from * around.
Rep rnd 1 until cuff measures 2"/5cm from cast-on edge (approx 16 rnds). Change to size 6 (4mm) needle.

LACE
Rnds 1, 3 and 5 *P2, k2, yo, k2tog, (p2, k1) twice; rep from * around.
Rnds 2, 4 and 6 *P2, ssk, yo, k2, (p2, k1) twice; rep from * around.
Rnd 7 *p2, C4F, (p2, k1) twice; rep from * around.
Rnd 8 Rep rnd 2.
Rnds 9, 11 and 13 *P2, k2, yo, k2tog; rep from * around.
Rnds 10, 12 and 14 *P2, ssk, yo, k2; rep from * around.
Rnd 15 *P2, k2, yo, k2tog, p2, C4F; rep from * around.
Rnd 16 Rep rnd 10.
Rnd 17 (inc rnd) *P1, m1, p1, k2, yo, k2tog; rep from * around—126 sts.
Rnds 18, 20 and 22 *P3, ssk, yo, k2; rep from * around.
Rnds 19 and 21 *P3, k2, yo, k2tog; rep from * around.

Gauges
21 sts and 31 rows to 4"/10cm over St st using larger needles.
19 sts and 30 rows to 4"/10cm over pat St using larger needles. *Take time to check gauges.*

Drawstring Cowl/Hat

Rnd 31 *P5, k2, yo, k2tog, p5 , C4F; rep from * around.

Rnd 32 *p5, ssk, yo, k2; rep from * around.

Rnd 33 (inc rnd) *P2, M1, p1, M1, p2, k2, yo, k2tog; rep from * around— 198 sts.

Rnd 34 *P7, ssk, yo, k2; rep from * around.

Rnd 35 (eyelet rnd) *P3, yo, p2tog, p2, k2, yo, k2tog; rep from * around.

Rnds 37–42 *P3, k1, p3, k1, p2, k1, rep from * around.

Bind off all sts. Weave in ends.

Finishing

I-CORD DRAWSTRING

With size 5 (3.75) needle, cast on 2 sts.
Work I-cord for 24"/61cm.
Weave in all ends.

TO WEAR AS A HAT

Thread I-cord drawstring through eyelets at top of hat (wider end of tube).
Cinch to tighten, then tie firmly in a bow to secure.

TO WEAR AS A COWL

Remove drawstring if it is threaded through eyelets at top of hat. Pull tube completely over head so that ribbed cuff lies around neck with the wider end of the tube resting on the shoulders. ■

✳ Thread the drawstring through the top row of eyelets and cinch to wear it as a hat!

Rnd 23 *P3, C4F, p3, k2, yo, k2tog; rep from * around.

Rnd 24 *P3, ssk, yo, k2; rep from * around.

Rnd 25 (inc rnd) *P1, (M1, p1) twice, k2, yo, k2tog; rep from * around—162 sts.

Rnds 26, 28 and 30 *P5, ssk, yo, k2; rep from * around.

Rnds 27 and 29 *P5, k2, yo, k2tog; rep from * around.

Checkered Mittens

Worked in two shades of green and accented with beige checks, these classic mittens make a great gift for a man or a woman. Wear them for a walk in the woods or a game of checkers on a chilly day.

DESIGNED BY LOIS S. YOUNG

Size
Instructions are written for Women's medium.

Knitted Measurements
Hand Circumference 7.5"/19cm
Length 10.25"/26cm

Materials
■ 1 1¾ oz/50g hank (each approx 164yd/150m) of *Cascade 220 Sport* (Peruvian highland wool) each in #9429 mossy rock (MC), #8021 beige (A), and #9430 highland green (B)

■ One set (5) size 6 (4mm) double-pointed needles (dpns) *or size to obtain gauge*

■ Stitch marker

■ Waste yarn

Pattern Stitch
Rnds 1, 2, 8, 9, 10, 11, 17 and 18 Using MC, knit.
Rnds 3, 4, 15 and 16 *K2 MC, k2 A; rep from * around.
Rnds 5 and 14 Using B, knit.
Rnds 6, 7, 12 and 13 *K2 A, k2 MC; rep from * around.
Rep rnds 1–18 for pat st.

Mitten (make 2)
CUFF
Using B, loosely cast on 48 sts. Place marker and join, being careful not to twist. Work 2 rnds k2, p2 ribbing. Change to A and work 1 rnd K2, P2 rib. Change to MC and work K2, P2 rib until cuff measures 3"/7.5cm.

HAND
Work rnds 1–18 of pat st, then work rnd 1 once more.
Next rnd Working rnd 2 of pat, work 2 sts, then work next 9 sts using a piece of waste yarn for thumb. Slip these 9 sts back to the LH needle and k them once again in MC; work to end of rnd. Cont in pat until Rnds 1–18 of pattern have been worked twice, then work rnds 1–13 once more.
Rnd 14 Using B, k2tog around—24 sts.
Rnds 15 and 16 *K1 MC, k1 A; rep from * around.

Rnd 17 Using MC, k2tog around—12 sts.
Last rnd Using MC, k2tog around—6 sts. Break yarn, leaving 5"/12.5cm end. Pull yarn through sts and fasten off.

THUMB
Carefully remove waste yarn from thumb opening, putting 9 sts from bottom of thumb opening on one needle and the 8 sts from top on a second needle. Starting with bottom needle and MC, k9, pick up and k 1 st from side of opening, k8 from second needle, pick up and k2 sts from side opening, place marker—20 sts. Arrange sts so they are evenly divided on needles. Cont with rnd 3 of pat, lining up pat on bottom of thumb; pat on top will be one st off. Cont until rnd 18 is completed, work rnds 1–3.
Next rnd 4 *K2tog, MC, k2 tog A; rep from * around—10 sts.
Next rnd 5 *Using B, k2 tog, k3; rep from * around—8 sts.
Last rnd Using MC, k2tog around—4 sts. Break yarn leaving a 3"/7.5cm end. Pull yarn through sts and fasten off.

Finishing
Weave in all ends. Use beg of thumb yarn to neaten any holes caused by picking up sts for thumb. Block lightly to measurements. ■

Gauge
25 sts and 27 rnds to 4"/10cm over pat st using size 6 (4mm) needles. *Take time to check gauge.*

Puppy Hat

This adorable, fun-to-knit topper will have you wagging your tail in no time.
Customize the colors to match your favorite pooch.

DESIGNED BY LOIS S. YOUNG

Size
Instructions are written for one size.

Knitted Measurements
Head circumference 20"/51cm
Depth 8½"/21.5cm

Materials
- 1 1¾oz/50g hank (each approx 164yd/150m) of *Cascade 220 Sport* (Peruvian highland wool) each in #8021 beige (MC), #2450 mystic purple (A), #9408 cordovan (B) and #9477 tutu (C)
- Size 7 (4.5mm) circular needle, 16"/40cm long *or size to obtain gauge*
- One set (5) size 7 (4.5mm) double-pointed needles (dpns)
- Stitch markers
- Sewing needle and contrasting sewing thread

Hat
With circular needle and A, cast on 100 sts. Join and pm, taking care not to twist sts on needle.

BRIM
Rnds 1 and 3 P.
Rnds 2 and 4 K.
Rnd 5 P. Change to MC.
Rnd 6 K.
Rnd 7 P. Change to B.
Rnds 8 and 9 Rep rnds 6 and 7. Change to A.
Rnds 10–21 K. Change to B.
Rnds 22 and 23 Rep rnds 6 and 7.

Change to MC.
Rnds 24 and 25 Rep rnds 6 and 7. Change to A.
Rnds 26 and 27 Rep rnds 6 and 7. Change to MC. Cont in St st (k every rnd) until piece measures 5¼"/13.5cm from beg.

TOP OF HEAD SHAPING
Dec rnd 1 *K8, ssk; rep from * around— 90 sts. K next 3 rnds.
Dec rnd 2 *K7, ssk; rep from around—80 sts. K next 3 rnds.
Dec rnd 3 *K14, ssk; rep from * around—75 sts. You will now be working back and forth in rows as foll:
Next row (RS) K10, pm, ssk; turn.
Next row Sl 1, p19, pm, p2tog; turn.
Next row Sl 1, k19, sl marker, ssk; turn.
Next row Sl 1, p19, sl marker, p2tog; turn. Rep last 2 rows 9 times more—53 sts. Change to dpns, dividing sts evenly over 4 needles.
Next rnd K, dropping head shaping markers.

NOSE AND MOUTH SHAPING
Dec rnd 1 K9, k2tog, k7, k2tog, k14, ssk, k7, ssk, k8—49 sts. K next rnd.
Dec rnd 2 K8, k2tog, k6, k2tog, k14, ssk, k6, ssk, k7—45 sts. K next rnd.
Dec rnd 3 K7, k2tog, k5, k2tog, k4, [k2tog] 3 times, k4, ssk, k5, ssk, k6—38

Gauge
20 sts and 28 rnds to 4"/10cm over St st using size 7 (4.5mm) circular needle. *Take time to check gauge.*

sts. K next rnd.

Dec rnd 4 K6, k2tog, k4, k2tog, k11, ssk, k4, ssk, k5—34 sts. K next rnd.

Dec rnd 5 K5, k2tog, k3, k2tog, k11, ssk, k3, ssk, k4—30 sts. K next rnd.

Dec rnd 6 K4, k2tog, k7, k2tog, k1, ssk, k7, ssk, k3—26 sts. K next rnd.

Dec rnd 7 K3, k2tog, k17, ssk, k2—24 sts. K next rnd.

Dec rnd 8 K5, k2tog, k2, k2tog, k3, ssk, k2, ssk, k4—20 sts. K next rnd.

Dec rnd 9 K2, [k2tog] 4 times, [ssk] 4 times, k2—12 sts.

Dec rnd 10 [K2tog] 3 times, [ssk] 3 times—6 sts. Cut yarn leaving a 6"/15cm tail and thread through rem sts. Pull tog tightly and secure end.

Ears (make 2)

With dpns and 2 strands of B held tog, cast on 11 sts. Working back and forth on 2 dpns, work even in garter st (k every row) for 29 rows. Shape bottom of ear as foll:

Dec row 1 K1, ssk, k to last 3 sts, k2tog, k1—9 sts. K next row. Rep last 2 rows twice more—5 sts.

Dec row 2 Ssk, k1, k2tog—3 sts. Bind off kwise.

Nose

With dpns and 2 strands of B held tog, cast on 9 sts. Working back and forth on 2 dpns, work as foll:

Rows 1 and 3 (WS) Sl 1 wyib, p to end.

Row 2 Sl 1 wyib, k to end.

Shape nose as foll:

Row (dec) 4 Sl 1 wyib, ssk, k to last 3 sts, k2tog, k1—7 sts.

Rows 5 Sl 1 wyib, p to end.

Row (dec) 6 Sl 1 wyib, ssk, k to last 3 sts, k2tog, k1—5 sts.

Row 7 Rep row 5.

Row (dec) 8 Ssk, k1, k2tog—3 sts. Bind off pwise.

Tongue

With dpns and 2 strands of C held tog, cast on 9 sts. Working back and forth on 2 dpns, work even in garter st for 13 rows. Shape tip of tongue as foll:

Dec row 1 K1, ssk, k to last 3 sts, k2tog, k1—7 sts. Kn next row. Rep last 2 rows once more—5 sts.

Dec row 2 Ssk, k1, k2tog—3 sts. Bind off kwise.

Finishing

NOSE

Cut a 36"/91.5cm length of B for stuffing; set aside. Position nose on top of head, so tip of nose is even with last rnd of head. Using 1 strand of B, sew side edges in place leaving last side open. Stuff with reserved yarn, then sew opening closed.

TONGUE

On underside of head (opposite nose), position cast-on edge of tongue 1¾"/4.5cm from last rnd of head. Using 1 strand of C, sew cast-on edge in place.

EARS

Pin cast-on edge of each ear to side of head, so top corner of ear is at beg of head shaping and side edge of ear runs parallel to bottom edge of hat. Using 1 strand of B, sew cast-on edge in place.

EYES

Using sewing needle and thread, sew a horizontal row of running stitches 1¼"/3cm up from top edge of nose to indicate bottom edge of eyes. Sew another horizontal row of running stitches 1⅛"/2.8cm up from first row of running stitches to indicate top edge of eyes. Referring to actual-size pattern, outline eyes in backstitch using 1 strand of B. Embroider pupils in long and short vertical satin stitches using 1 strand of B. Remove sewing thread stitches. ∎

Eyes

Fringed Scarf

With its subtle, ribbed pattern, this scarf is an ideal accessory for men and women alike. Fringed ends give it added flair.

DESIGNED BY LOIS S. YOUNG

Size
Instructions are written for one size.

Knitted Measurements
Approx 8" x 63"/20.5cm x 160cm (excluding fringe)

Materials
■ 4 1¾oz/50g hanks (each approx 164yd/150m) of *Cascade 220 Sport* (Peruvian highland wool) in #2401 burgundy

■ One pair size 6 (4mm) needles *or size to obtain gauge*

■ Size G/6 (4mm) crochet hook (for fringe)

Scarf
Cast on 49 sts. Cont in fancy rib st as foll:

Rows 1, 3, 5 and 7 (RS) Sl 1, k2, *p3, [k1, p1] twice, k1; rep from *, end p3, k2, k1 tbl.

Rows 2, 4, 6 and 8 Sl 1, k2, *k3, p5; rep from *, end k5, k1 tbl.

Row 9 Rep row 1.

Rows 10, 12, 14 and 16 Sl 1, k2, *p4, k3, p1; rep from *, end p3, k2, k1 tbl.

Rows 11, 13, 15 and 17 Sl 1, k2, *[p1, k1] twice, p3, k1; rep from *, end p1, k1, p1, k2, k1 tbl.

Row 18 Rep row 10. Rep rows 1–18 twenty-five times more, then rows 1–8 once. Bind off knitwise.

Finishing
Block piece lightly to measurements.

FRINGE
Cut 12"/30.5cm strands of yarn. Using 2 strands for each fringe, attach 24 fringes, evenly spaced across each end of scarf. Trim ends evenly. ■

Gauge
24 sts and 30 rows to 4"/10cm over fancy rib st using size 6 (4mm) needles (after blocking). *Take time to check gauge..*

Art Deco Mittens

Evoking such classic Art Deco designs as the Empire State Building and the Chrysler Building, these jewel-toned mittens are timeless. The corrugated cuffs and intricate Fair Isle pattern make them a fun challenge to knit.

DESIGNED BY STEPHANIE EARP

Size
Instructions are written for one size.

Knitted Measurements
Hand Circumference 8"/20cm
Length 9¼"/23.5cm

Materials
■ 1 1¾oz/50g hank (each approx 164yd/150m) of *Cascade 220 Sport* (Peruvian highland wool) each in #8892 azure (MC) and #9451 lake-chelan heather (CC)

■ One set (5) size 4 (3.5mm) double-pointed needles (dpns) or size to obtain gauge

■ Scrap yarn

■ Stitch marker

Stitch Glossary
M1 Inc 1 st by casting on 1 st using backward-loop method.

Right Mitten
With MC, cast on 40 sts. Place marker (pm) and join, being careful not to twist sts.
Rnd 1 *K1 MC, p1 CC; rep from * around. Rep rnd 1 for corrugated ribbing until cuff measures 1¾"/4.5cm from beg.
Next (inc) rnd *K2, M1, K3, M1, k3, M1, k2, M1, k2, M1, k3, M1, k3, M1, K2; rep from * around—54 sts.

BEG CHART I
Work foll chart until rnd 17 is complete.

THUMB PLACEMENT
Rnd 18 (thumb opening) Work 31 sts in chart pat, then with scrap yarn, k next 9 sts, sl these 9 sts back to LH needle, and work them again foll chart. Cont to foll chart until 54 rnds are complete—26 sts rem.
Cut yarns, leaving a 15"/38cm tail in MC. Thread tail on darning needle and run yarn through rem sts twice. Pull tight to close.

THUMB
Carefully remove scrap yarn and place live sts from upper and lower edges of opening evenly on 4 dpns—18 sts.

BEG CHART II
Next rnd With RS facing and MC, beg at lower edge of thumb opening and pick up and k 1 st, then, beg with st 2, work rnd 1 of chart through st 10, with MC pick up and k 1 st, cont to foll to end of rnd—20 sts. Cont to foll chart until rnd 17 is complete—12 sts. Cut yarns, leaving a 12"/30.5cm tail in MC. Thread MC on darning needle and run yarn through rem sts twice. Pull tight to close.

Left Mitten
Work same as for right mitten until chart rnd 17 is complete.

THUMB PLACEMENT
Rnd 18 (thumb opening) Work 41 sts in chart pat, then with scrap yarn, k next 9 sts, sl these 9 sts back to LH needle, and work them again foll chart.
Complete as for right mitten, working chart 3 for thumb. ■

Gauge
26 sts and 28 rnds to 4"/10cm over stranded colorwork using size 4 (3.5mm) needles.
Take time to check gauge.

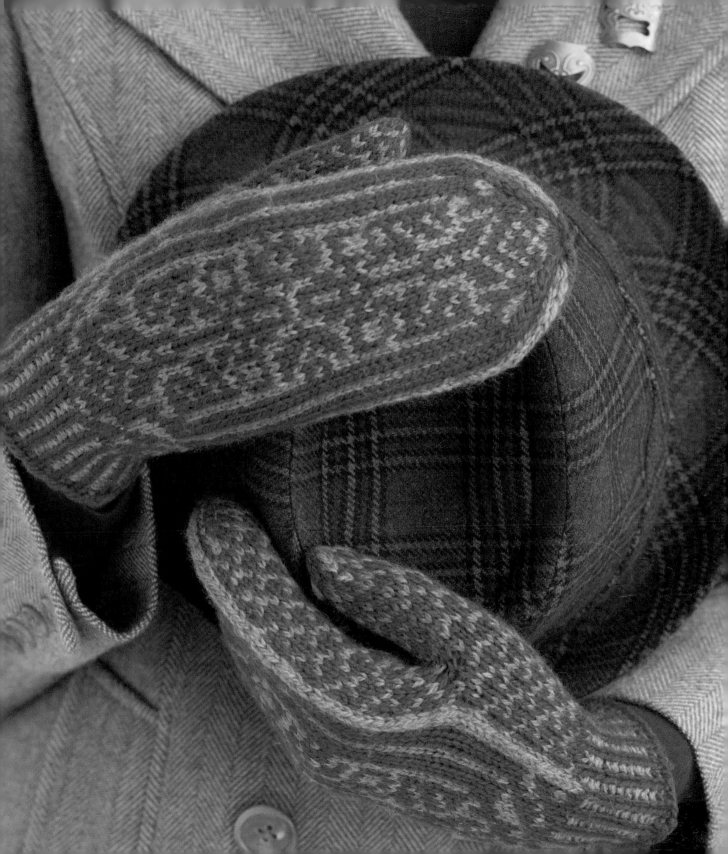

Art Deco Mittens

CHART II

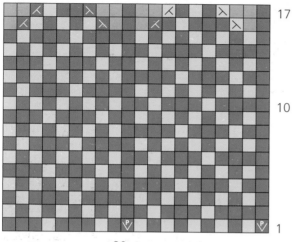

17

10

1

20 sts

CHART III

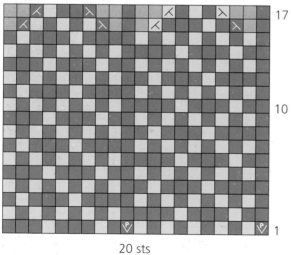

17

10

1

20 sts

Stitch Key

 Ssk

K2tog

Pick up and knit

No stitch

Knit

Color Key

Azure (MC)

Lake Chelan Heather (CC)

CHART I

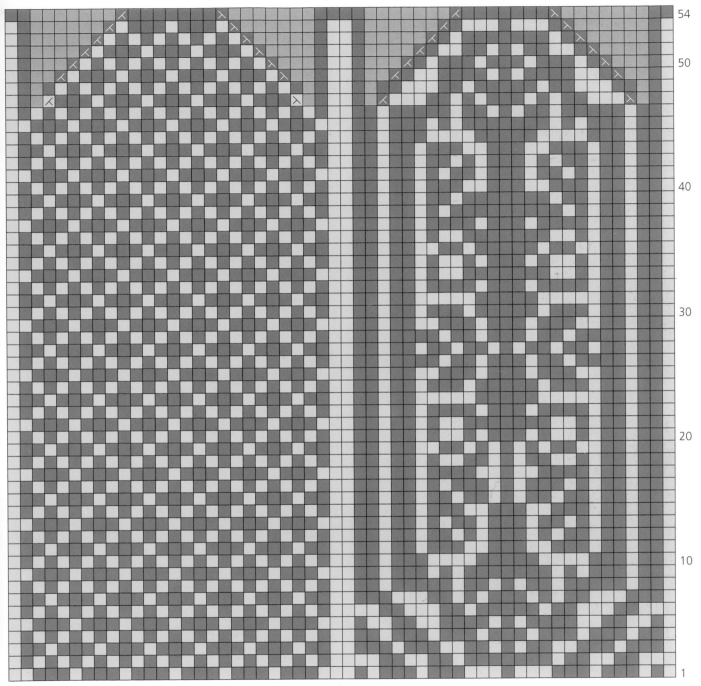

54 sts

Woven Ribs Muffler

Ready to move beyond a basic garter-stitch scarf? Cast on for this textured basketweave-and-ribbed design, ideal for both the guys and the gals on your gift list.

DESIGNED BY LYNN M. WILSON

Size
Instructions are written for one size.

Knitted Measurements
Width at ends 7.5"/19cm
Width in center 5.5"/14cm to 6"/15cm
Length 68"/172.5cm

Materials
■ 4 1¾ oz/50g hanks (each approx. 164yd/150m) of *Cascade 220 Sport* (Peruvian highland wool) in #9451 lake chelan heather

■ One pair size 5 (3.75mm) needles *or size to obtain gauge*

Note
For a variation on the design, work fewer or more repeats of the k2 p2 ribbing between each band of garter stitch & ribs or work fewer or more repeats of the garter stitch & ribs pattern at the ends.

Stitch Glossary
GARTER STITCH & RIBS PATTERN
Row 1, 3, 5 and 7 (RS) K5, *p2, k10; rep from * to last 7 sts, p2, k5.
Rows 2, 4, 6 and 8 (WS) K3, *p2, k2, p2, k6; rep from * to last 9 sts, p2, k2, p2, k3.
Rows 9, 11, 13 and 15 K11, *p2, k10; *rep from * to last st, k1.
Rows 10, 12, 14 and 16 K9, *p2, k2, p2, k6; rep from * to last 3 sts, k3.
Rep rows 1–16 for garter st & ribs pat.

KNIT 2, PURL 2 RIBBING
Row 1 (RS) K5, p2, *k2, p2; rep from * to last 5 sts, k5.
Row 2 K3, *p2, k2; rep from * to last 5 sts, p2, k3.
Rep rows 1 and 2 for k2, p2 rib.

Muffler
Cast on 48 sts and work rows 1–16 of garter st & ribs pat 4 times, then work rows 1–8 once more.
For center portion of the muffler, work sections 1 & 2 as foll:
SECTION 1
Work rows 1 & 2 of k2, p2 rib for 10"/25.5cm, end with a WS row.
SECTION 2
Work rows 1–8 of garter st & ribs pat. Rep sections 1 & 2 three times more; then rep section 1 once more.
Work rows 1–16 of garter st & ribs pat 4 times; then work Rows 1–8 once more. Bind off purlwise.

Finishing
Block lightly to measurements. ■

Gauges
24 sts and 34 rows to 4"/10cm over garter st & ribs pat using size 5 (3.75mm) needles. 22 sts and 28 rows to 4"/10cm over St st using size 5 (3.75mm) needles. *Take time to check gauges.*

Diamond-Pattern Mittens

A black-and-gray Fair Isle pattern creates a graphic statement in these toasty mitts. Twisted-rib cuffs keep them snug.

DESIGNED BY YOKO HATTA

Size
Instructions are written for one size.

Knitted Measurements
Hand circumference 7¾"/19.5cm
Length 11"/28cm

Materials
■ 1 1¾oz/50g hanks (each approx 164yd/150m) of *Cascade 220 Sport* (Peruvian highland wool) each in #4002 jet (MC) and #8401 silver grey (CC)

■ One set (5) size 6 (4mm) and size 5 (3.75mm) double-pointed needles (dpns) *or size to obtain gauge*

■ One set (5) size 4 (3.5mm) double-pointed needles (dpns)

■ Stitch markers

■ Waste yarn

Stitch Glossary
TWISTED 1X1 RIB
(multiple of 2 sts)
Rnd 1 *P1, k1 tbl; rep from * around.
Rep rnd 1 for pat.

Mitten Cuff
With size 4 needles and MC, cast on 48 sts. Join and pm, taking care not to twist sts on needle. Work in twisted 1X1 rib for a total of 24 rnds. Change to size 6 needles. With MC, knit 1 rnd. Beg color chart, working 2 repeats of chart around and stranding color not in use loosely on WS of work. Work in pat for 16 rnds.

Left Mitten
THUMB OPENING
Next rnd Work in color pat as set for 16 sts. With waste yarn, knit across next 8 sts; return sts to left needle and knit across in pat; work as set to end of rnd.

TOP OF HAND
Cont chart for a total of 52 rnds—4 sts. Graft rem sts using Kitchener stitch.

Right Mitten
THUMB OPENING
Next rnd With waste yarn, knit across next 8 sts; return sts to left needle and knit across in pat; work as set to end of rnd.

TOP OF HAND
Work as for left mitten.

THUMB
Carefully cut waste yarn and place 17 live sts (8 below and 9 above opening) on needles. With size 5 needles and MC, pick up and knit 1 st in corner of opening, knit across 8 live sts, pick up and knit 1 st in corner of opening, knit across 9 live sts—19 sts. Join and pm. Work even in St st for 21 rnds.
Next rnd *K2tog; rep from * to last st, k1—10 sts. Cut yarn leaving an 8"/20.5cm tail and thread through rem sts. Pull tog tightly and secure end.

Finishing
Block piece lightly to measurements. ■

Gauges
25 sts and 28 rnds to 4"/10cm over St st using size 5 (3.75mm) needles. 25 sts and 26 rnds to 4"/10cm over stranded color pat using size 6 (4mm) needles. *Take time to check gauges.*

Diamond-Pattern Mittens

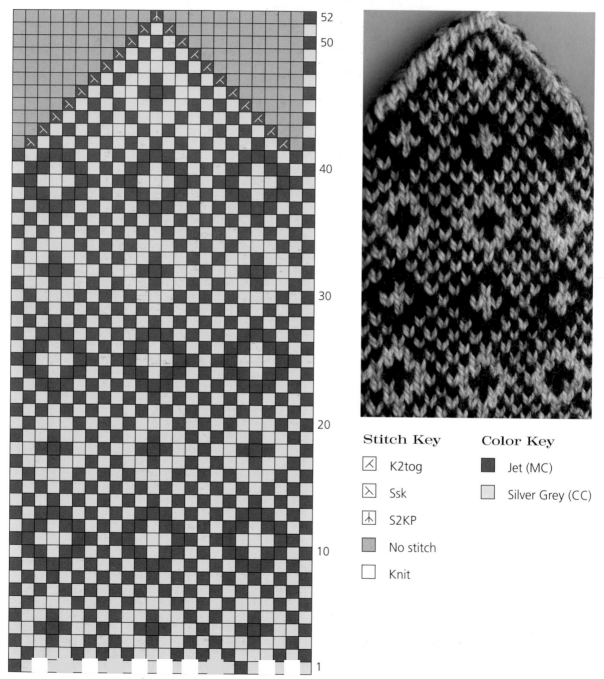

24 sts

Stitch Key

⊠ K2tog

⊠ Ssk

⅄ S2KP

▨ No stitch

☐ Knit

Color Key

■ Jet (MC)

☐ Silver Grey (CC)

Fair Isle Tam

Beginning with a ribbed brim, this tam is increased out then decreased back in while staying in pattern. Keep things simple with two colors and watch the beauty unfold.

DESIGNED BY HEIDI TODD KOZAR

Size
Instructions are written for one size.

Knitted Measurements
Head circumference 20"/51cm
Diameter 12"/30.5cm

Materials
■ 1 1¾oz/50g hank (each approx 164yd/150m) of *Cascade 220 Sport* (Peruvian highland wool) each in #2450 mystic purple (MC) and, #8393 navy (CC)

■ Sizes 4 and 6 (3.5 and 4mm) circular needles, 16"/40cm long *or size to obtain gauge*

■ One set (5) size 6 (4mm) double-pointed needles (dpns)

■ Stitch marker

Corrugated Rib
(multiple of 4 sts)
Rnd 1 *K2 with CC, p2 with MC; rep from * around.
Rep rnd 1 for corrugated rib.

Tam
With smaller circular needle and MC, cast on 136 sts. Join and pm, taking care not to twist sts on needle. Cont in corrugated rib and work even for 2"/5cm.
Next rnd With MC, k.
Next (inc) rnd With MC, *[K4, M1, k3, M1] 8 times, [k3, M1] 4 times; rep from * around—176 sts.

Gauge
24 sts and 28 rnds to 4"/10cm over St st and chart pats using larger circular needle. *Take time to check gauge.*

Fair Isle Tam

CHART I

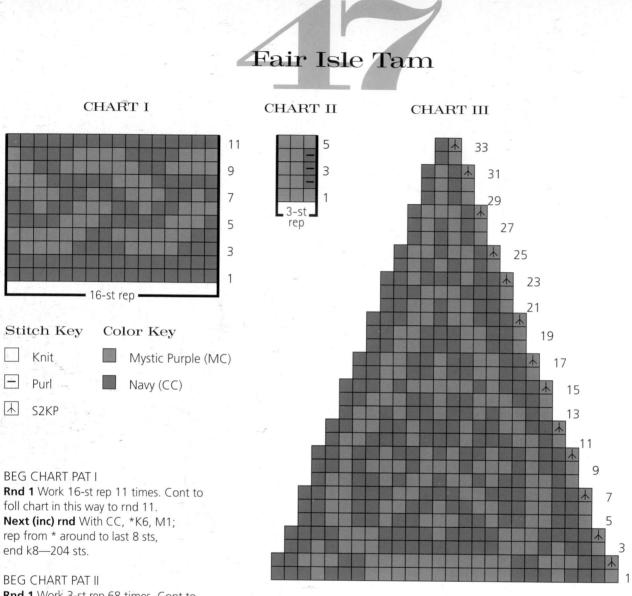

11
9
7
5
3
1

16-st rep

CHART II

5
3
1

3-st rep

CHART III

33
31
29
27
25
23
21
19
17
15
13
11
9
7
5
3
1

26 sts

Stitch Key

☐ Knit

⊟ Purl

⊼ S2KP

Color Key

Mystic Purple (MC)

Navy (CC)

BEG CHART PAT I
Rnd 1 Work 16-st rep 11 times. Cont to foll chart in this way to rnd 11.
Next (inc) rnd With CC, *K6, M1; rep from * around to last 8 sts, end k8—204 sts.

BEG CHART PAT II
Rnd 1 Work 3-st rep 68 times. Cont to foll chart in this way to rnd 5.
Next rnd With CC, k.
Next (inc) rnd With CC, k inc 4 sts evenly spaced—208 sts.

BEG CHART PAT III
Change to dpns (dividing sts evenly between 4 needles) when there are too few sts on circular needle.
Rnd 1 Work 26-st rep 8 times.

Rnd (dec) 2 Remove rnd marker, sl last st on RH needle to LH needle, pm on RH needle to indicate new beg of rnds. Cont to work rnd 2 of chart—132 sts. Cont to work to top of chart, moving marker every dec rnd (same as rnd 2)—16 sts. Cut CC.
Next (dec) rnd With MC, [k2tog] 8 times—8 sts. Cut yarn leaving a 6"/15cm

tail. Thread tail in tapestry needle, then thread through rem sts. Pull tog tightly and secure end. Weave in CC.

Finishing
Stretch beret over a 12"/30.5cm diameter dinner plate or heavy cardboard circle. Steam-block; let dry. ◼

Mitered Squares Scarf

It's hip to be square! A great introduction to the mitering technique, this scarf will have you mastering the skill in a flash.

DESIGNED BY MARY BETH TEMPLE

■◖■■◗

Size
Instructions are written for one size.

Knitted Measurements
Approx 8" x 74"/20.5cm x 188cm

Materials
■ 3 1¾oz/50g hanks (each approx 164yd/150m) of *Cascade 220 Sport* (Peruvian highland wool) in #8885 dark plum (A)

■ 1 hank each in #2450 mystic purple (B) and #2452 turtle (C)

■ One pair size 6 (4mm) needles *or size to obtain gauge*

■ Size E/4 (3.5mm) crochet hook

Note
Scarf is made in two panels, then sewn tog.

Scarf Panel (make 2)
Note Refer to chart for color placement, and where and how squares are joined.

SQUARE 1
With A, cast on 41 sts.
Row 1 (WS) Purl.
Row 2 (RS) K19, SK2P, k19—39 sts.
Row 3 Purl.
Row 4 Knit to one st before dec, SK2P, knit to end.
Row 5 Purl. Rep rows 4 and 5 until 3 sts rem, end with a WS row.
Last row SK2P. Fasten off last st.

SQUARE 2
With B, cast on 11 sts, then pick up and k 10 sts halfway up RH edge of square 1—21 sts.
Row 1 (WS) Purl.
Row 2 (RS) K9, SK2P, k9—19 sts.
Row 3 Purl.
Row 4 Knit to one st before dec, SK2P, knit to end.
Row 5 Purl. Rep rows 4 and 5 until 3 sts rem, end with a WS row.
Last row SK2P. Fasten off last st.

SQUARE 3
With RS facing and C, pick up and k 10 sts along top edge of square 2, pick up and k 1 st in intersection of square 1 and square 2, then pick up and k 10 sts along rem RH edge of square 1—21 sts. Cont to work same as square 2.

SQUARE 4
With RS facing and B (and beg in center top edge of square 1), pick up and k 10 sts along top edge of square 1, then cast on 11 sts—21 sts. Cont to work same as square 2.

SQUARE 5
With RS facing and C, pick up and k 10 sts along top edge of square 4, then cast on 11 sts—21 sts. Cont to work same as square 2.

SQUARE 6
With RS facing and A, pick up and k 20 sts along top edges of square 3 and square 1, pick up and k 1 st at the intersection of square 1 and square 4, then pick up and k 20 sts along side edges of square 4 and square 5—41 sts. Cont to work same as square 1.

Gauge
18 sts and 30 rows to 4"/10cm over St st using size 6 (4mm) needles. *Take time to check gauge.*

Mitered Squares Scarf

SQUARE 7
With RS facing and A (and beg in center top edge of square 6), pick up 20 sts along top edge of square 6 and square 5, then cast on 21 sts—41 sts. Cont to work same as square 1.

SQUARE 8
With RS facing and B, pick up and k 10 sts along top edge of square 6, pick up and k 1 st in intersection of square 6 and square 7, then pick up and k 10 sts half way up RH edge of square 7—21 sts. Cont to work same as square 2.

SQUARE 9
With RS facing and C, pick up and k 10 sts along top edge of square 8, pick up and k 1 st in intersection of square 8 and square 7, then pick up and k 10 sts along rem RH edge of square 7—21 sts. Cont to work same as square 2. Cont adding squares foll chart for color placement.

Finishing
Sew top edges of panels tog using A.

EDGING
With RS facing and crochet hook, join A with a sl st in side edge of sewn seam.
Rnd 1 (RS) Ch 1, sc evenly around entire outer edge, working 3 sc in each corner, join rnd with a sl st in first sc.
Rnd 2 (RS) Ch 1, sc in each st around, working 3 sc in each corner st, join rnd with a sl st in first sc. Fasten off. Block piece to measurements. ■

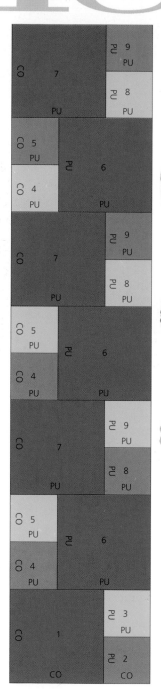

Color Key
■ Dark Plum (A)
■ Mystic Purple (B)
□ Turtle (C)

Abbreviations
CO Cast on

PU Pick up

Cabled Gauntlets

Add a little flare to your winter wardrobe with these all-over cabled mittens. Increasing and decreasing while cabling will keep your interest, and the extra-long cuffs will keep your wrists extra-warm!

DESIGNED BY MARY BETH TEMPLE

Size
Instructions are written for one size.

Knitted Measurements
Hand circumference 7"/18cm
Length of cuff Approx 4½"/11.5cm

Materials
■ 2 1¾oz/50g hanks (each approx 164yd/150m) of *Cascade 220 Sport* (Peruvian highland wool) in #9326 colonial blue heather

■ One set (5) size 4 (3.5mm) double-pointed needles (dpns) *or size to obtain gauge*

■ Cable needle (cn)

■ Stitch markers

Stitch Glossary
4-st RC Sl 2 sts to cn and hold to *back*, k2, k2 from cn.

4-st LC Sl 2 sts to cn and hold to *front*, k2, k2 from cn.

3-st RC Dec Sl 2 sts to cn and hold to *back*, ssk, k2 from cn.

kf&b Inc 1 by knitting into the front and back of the next st.

Cable Pattern
(multiple of 6 sts)
Rnd 1 *K2, 4-st LC; rep from * around.
Rnds 2–4 Knit.
Rnd 5 *4-st RC, k2; rep from * around.
Rnds 6–8 Knit.
Rep rnds 1–8 for cable pat.

Mitten (make 2)
CUFF
With dpns, cast on 78 sts. Divide sts over 4 needles. Join taking care not to twist sts on needles, pm for beg of rnds. Cont in cable rib pat as foll:

Rnds 1, 3 and 5 Purl.
Rnds 2 and 4 Knit.
Rnds 6–8 *[K6, p5] 3 times, k6; rep from * around.
Rnd 9 *[K2, 4-st LC, p5] 3 times, k2, 4-st LC; rep from * around.
Rnds 10–12 Rep rnd 6.
Rnd 13 *[4-st RC, k2, p5] 3 times, 4-st RC, k2; rep from * around.
Rnds 14–16 Rep rnd 6.
Rnd 17 Rep rnd 9.
Rnd (dec) 18 *K5, ssk, p3, k2tog, [k4, ssk, p3, k2tog] twice, k5; rep from * around—66 sts.
Rnds 19–20 *[K6, p3] 3 times, k6; rep from * around.
Rnd 21 *[4-st RC, k2, p3] 3 times, 4-st RC, k2; rep from * around.
Rnds 22–24 Rep rnd 19.
Rnd 25 *[K2, 4-st LC, p3] twice, k2, 4-st LC; rep from * around.
Rnds 26–28 Rep rnd 19.
Rnds 29–32 Rep rnds 21–24.
Rnd 33 Rep rnd 25.
Rnd (dec) 34 *K5, ssk, p1, k2tog, [k4, ssk, p1, k2tog] twice, k5; rep from * around—54 sts.
Rnds 35–36 *[K6, p1] 3 times, k6; rep from * around.

Gauge
27 sts and 30 rnds to 4"/10cm over cable pat using size 4 (3.5mm) dpns. *Take time to check gauge.*

Cabled Gauntlets

Rnd 37 *[4-st RC, k2, p1] 3 times, 4-st RC, k2; rep from * around.
Rnd 38 Rep rnd 35.
Rnd (dec) 39 *[K5, ssk] 3 times, k6; rep from * around—48 sts.
Rnd 40 Knit. Work rnds 1–8 of cable pat. Cont in cable pat and work thumb gusset as foll:

THUMB GUSSET

Rnd 1 K2, pm, k2, pm, k2, *k2, 4-st LC; rep from * around.
Rnds 2–4 Knit.
Rnd 5 K2, sl marker, [kf&b] twice, sl marker, k2, *4-st RC, k2; rep from * to end—50 sts.
Rnds 6–8 Knit.
Rnd 9 K2, sl marker, kf&b, knit to st before marker, kf&b, sl marker, k2, *k2, 4-st LC; rep from * around—52 sts.
Rnds 10–12 Knit.
Rnd 13 K2, sl marker, kf&b, knit to st before marker, kf&b, sl marker, k2, *4-st RC, k2; rep from * around—54 sts.
Rnds 14–16 Knit.
Rnds 17–23 Rep rnds 9–15—58 sts (12 sts between thumb gusset markers).
Next rnd K2, drop marker, place next 12 sts on scrap for thumb, drop marker, cast on 2 sts, knit to end—48 sts.

HAND

Beg with rnd 1, cont in cable pat until piece measures 13"/33cm from beg, end with rnd 8.

TOP SHAPING

Dec rnd 1 *Ssk, 4-st LC; rep from * around—40 sts. Knit next rnd.
Dec rnd 2 *K3, ssk; rep from * around—32 sts. Knit next rnd.
Dec rnd 3 *3-st RC dec, k1; rep from * around—24 sts. Knit next rnd. Graft sts tog using Kitchener st or use 3-needle bind-off.

THUMB

Place 12 thumb gusset sts over 2 needles.
Next rnd Join yarn and knit across sts, then pick up and k 1 st before cast-on of thumb opening, 2 sts over cast-on of opening, then 1 st after cast-on of opening—16 sts. Divide sts evenly over 3 needles. Join and pm for beg of rnds. Cont in St st for 2"/5cm.

TOP SHAPING

Dec rnd 1 K1, *k1, k2tog; rep from * around—11 sts. Knit next rnd.
Dec rnd 2 K1, *k2tog; rep from * around— 6 sts. Cut yarn leaving a 6"/15cm tail and thread through rem sts. Pull tog tightly and secure end. ■

50 Convertible Mitten-Gloves

Are they gloves or are they mittens? Both! In this clever design, individual ribbed half-fingers tuck under a convertible flap, ideal for both cold hands and finger mobility.

DESIGNED BY YOKO HATTA

SIZE
Instructions are written for one size.

Knitted Measurements
Hand circumference 7½"/19cm
Length 12"/30.5 cm

Materials
■ 1 1¾oz/50g hanks (each approx 164yd/150m) of *Cascade 220 Sport* (Peruvian highland wool) each in #8400 charcoal grey (A), #9421 blue hawaii (B), #8914 granny smith (C), #7805 flamingo pink (D) and #7809 violet (E)

■ One set (5) size 6 (4mm) double-pointed needles (dpns) *or size to obtain gauge*

■ One set (5) size 4 (3.5mm) double-pointed needles (dpns)

■ Stitch markers

■ Stitch holders

■ Waste yarn

Stitch Glossary
2X2 RIB
Rnd 1 *K2, p2; rep from * around.
Rep rnd 1 for pat.

Note
Rnds beg with back of hand sts.

Mitt Cuff
With smaller needles and A, cast on 44 sts. Join and pm, taking care not to twist sts on needle. Work in 2X2 rib for 6 rnds. Change to B and work even in pat for 3 rnds. Cont in pat, changing colors every 3 rnds as follows: C, A, E, D. Change to A and work even in pat for 5 rnds. Cont in pat, changing colors every 3 rnds as follows: B, E, D, A.

Hand
Change to larger needles and B. Work in St st (knit every rnd) for 3 rnds. Cont in pat, changing colors every 3 rnds as follows: C, A, E, D, A.

Left Mitt
THUMB OPENING
With A, knit to last 7 sts. With waste yarn, knit across next 7 sts; return sts to left needle and with A, knit across to end of rnd. Cont with A, work even in St st for 16 rnds more. Cut yarn.

INDEX FINGER
With larger needles and B, knit across first 6 sts. Place next 32 sts on holder. Cast on 2 sts for gap, then knit last 6 sts—14 sts. Work in St st for 9 rnds. Bind off.

MIDDLE FINGER
With larger needles and C, knit across next 6 sts from holder. Cast on 2 sts for gap, then knit last 6 sts on opposite end of holder and pick up and knit 2 sts from base of index finger—16 sts. Work in St st for 9 rnds. Bind off.

Gauge
23 sts and 34 rnds to 4"/10cm over St st using size 6 (4mm) needles. *Take time to check gauge.*

Convertible Mitten-Gloves

RING FINGER

With larger needles and E, knit across next 5 sts from holder. Cast on 2 sts for gap, then knit last 5 sts on opposite end of holder and pick up and knit 2 sts from base of middle finger—14 sts.
Work in St st for 9 rnds. Bind off.

PINKY FINGER

With larger needles and D, knit across rem 10 sts from holder. Pick up and knit 2 sts from base of ring finger—12 sts.
Work in St st for 9 rnds. Bind off.

THUMB

Carefully cut waste yarn and place 15 live sts (7 below and 8 above opening) on needles. With larger needles and A, pick up and knit 1 st in corner of opening, knit across 7 live sts, pick up and knit 1 st in corner of opening, knit across 8 live sts—17 sts. Join and pm. Work even in St st for 25 rnds.
Next rnd *K2tog; rep from * to last st, k1—9 sts. Cut yarn leaving an 8"/20.5cm tail and thread through rem sts. Pull tog tightly and secure end.

Right Mitt

THUMB OPENING

With A, k22 back of hand sts. With waste yarn, knit across next 7 sts; return sts to left needle and with A, knit across and to end of rnd. Cont with A, work even in St st for 16 rnds more. Cut yarn.

FINGERS

Skip 22 back of hand sts, place new beg of rnd marker at thumb side of hand. Work fingers as for left mitt, beginning on palm side instead of back of hand.

THUMB

Work as for left mitt.

Hood (both mitts)

With larger needles and A, pick up and knit 22 sts across back of hand, 3 rnds below base of fingers. Cast on 24 sts more—46 sts. Join and pm taking care not to twist sts on needle. Work even in St st for 23 rnds.

SHAPE TOP

Rnd 1 *K1, ssk, k18, k2tog; rep from * on opposite side—42 sts.
Rnd 2 *K1, ssk, k16, k2tog; rep from * on opposite side—38 sts.
Rnd 3 *K1, ssk, k14, k2tog; rep from * on opposite side—34 sts.
Rnd 4 *K1, ssk, k12, k2tog; rep from * on opposite side—30 sts.
Rnd 5 *K1, ssk, k10, k2tog; rep from * on opposite side—26 sts.
Rnd 6 *K1, ssk, k8, k2tog; rep from * on opposite side—22 sts.
Rnd 7 *K1, ssk, k6, k2tog; rep from * on opposite side—18 sts.
Rnd 8 *K1, ssk, k4, k2tog; rep from * on opposite side—14 sts.
Rnd 9 *K1, ssk, k2, k2tog; rep from * on opposite side—10 sts.
Rnd 10 *K1, ssk, k2tog; rep from * on opposite side—6 sts. Graft rem sts using Kitchener stitch.

Finishing

Block piece lightly to measurements. ■

51

Lace Stole

Take your lace skills to the next level with this stunning scarf. With three lace charts worked across each row and a border of double-moss stitch, there's never a dull moment!

DESIGNED BY FAINA GOBERSTEIN

SIZE
Instructions are written for one size.

Knitted Measurements
Approx 15" x 60"/38.5cm x 152.5cm

Materials
■ 5 1¾oz/50g hanks (each approx 164yd/150m) of *Cascade 220 Sport* (Peruvian highland wool) in #9404 ruby
■ Two size 6 (4mm) circular needles, 29"/73cm *or size to obtain gauge*
■ Spare size 6 (4mm) needle (for 3-needle bind-off)
■ Stitch markers

Note
Shawl is made in two panels, then joined in the center using 3-needle bind-off.

Stitch Glossary
2–st RT K2tog leaving sts on LH needle, k first st again, sl both sts from needle.
2–st LT With RH needle behind LH needle, skip the first st and k 2nd st tbl, insert RH needle into backs of both sts, k2tog tbl.

Lace Panels (make 2)
With circular needle, cast on 95 sts. Cont in double moss st border pat as foll:
Row 1 (WS) Sl 1 wyif, [p2, k2] 11 times, p2, k1, [p2, k2], 11 times, p2, k1.

Row 2 (RS) Sl 1 wyif, [k2, p2] 11 times, k2, p1, [k2, p2] 11 times, k3.
Row 3 Rep row 2.
Row 4 Rep row 1. Rep rows 1–4 once more, then row 1 once.

BEG CHART PATS
Row 1 (RS) Sl 1 wyif, k2, p2, k2, pm, work chart I over next 30 sts, pm, work chart II over center 21 sts, pm, work chart III over next 30 sts, pm, k2 p2, k3.
Row 2 Sl 1 wyif, k2, p2, k2, sl marker, work chart III over next 30 sts, sl marker, work chart II over center 21 sts, sl marker, work chart I over next 30 sts, sl marker, k2, p2, k3. Keeping sts each side in double moss st border as established, cont to foll charts in this way, working to row 16 for charts I and III, and row 10 for chart II. Cont to rep rows 1–16 for charts I and III, and 1–10 for chart II until piece measures approx 30"/76cm from beg, end with row 10 of chart II. Leave sts on needle.

Finishing
With RS facing, hold panels tog on two parallel needles. Using third needle, cont to work 3–needle bind–off. Block piece lightly to measurements. ■

Gauge
27 sts and 28 rows to 4"/10cm over chart pats using size 6 (4mm) needle.
Take time to check gauge.

Lace Stole

CHART I

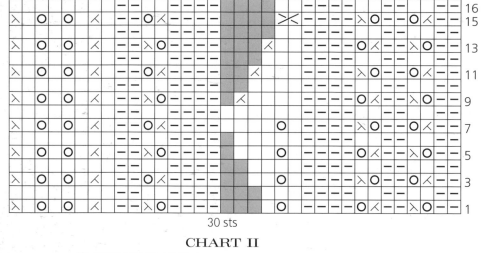

30 sts

CHART II

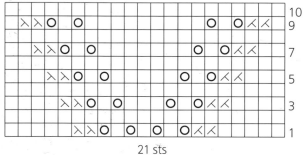

21 sts

CHART III

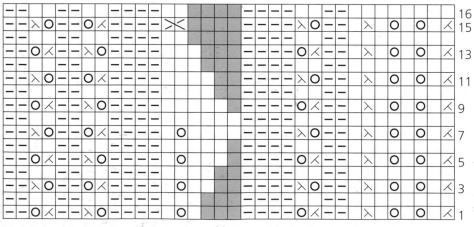

30 sts

Stitch Key

☐ K on RS, p on WS

─ P on RS, k on WS

⊙ Yarn over

╱ K2tog

╲ Ssk

⊠ 2-st RT

⊠ 2-st LT

▨ No stitch

Textured Fingerless Mitts

These unisex mitts feature two main stitch patterns—a wrapped rib stitch and the "modified Schiaparelli" pattern, from *The Complete Book of Knitting* by Barbara Abbey.

DESIGNED BY LORETTA DACHMAN

Size

Instructions are written for one size.

Measurements

Approx 2¾"/7cm across palm (unstretched)
Length 8¾"/22cm

Materials

■ 1 1¾oz/50g hank (each approx 164yd/150m) of *Cascade 220 Sport* (Peruvian highland wool) in #8892 azure

■ One set (5) size 5 (3.75mm) double-pointed needles (dpns) *or size to obtain gauge*

■ Stitch markers

■ Scrap yarn

Stitch Glossary

M1R With the needle tip, lift the strand between the last st k and the next st on the LH needle from the front and k into back of it. One k st has been added.
M1L With the needle tip, lift the strand between the last st worked and the next st on the LH needle from the back and k it. One k st has been added.

Rib Pattern

(multiple of 4 sts)
Rnds 1, 2 and 3 *K2, p2; rep from * around.
Rnd 4 *Yo, k2 and pull the yo over the k2, p2; rep from * around.
Rep rnds 1–4 for rib pat.

Modified Schiaparelli Pattern

Rnds 1 and 3 Knit.
Rnd 2 *Yo, k2 and pull the yo over the k2, k2; rep from * around.
Rnd 4 *K2, yo, k2 and pull the yo over the k2; rep from * around. Rep rnds 1–4 for modified Schiaparelli pattern.

Mitt 1

Cast on 44 sts for cuff. Join, being careful not to twist. Pm to mark beg of rnd. Work rib pat for 3"/7.5cm end rnd 3.

BEG THUMB GUSSET
Setup rnd Yo, k2 and pull the yo over the k2, pm, work rnd 4 of rib pattern over 20 sts (beginning with P2 or as established), work rnd 4 of modified Schiaparelli pat over 20 sts, p2.
Rnd 1 K to marker, sl marker, work pats as established, end P2.
Rnd 2 K1, M1R, k1, sl marker, work pats as established, end P2.
Rnds 3 and 4 Rep rnd 1.
Rnd 5 K1, M1R, k to 1 st before marker, M1L, k1, sl marker, work pats as established, end P2. Rep rnds 3–5 until there are a total of 15 sts before marker.
Next rnd K1, sl 13 sts to scrap yarn, k1 (pulling tightly to close any gap), work pats as established (incorporating two thumb sts into rib pat), end p2.
Work even until piece measures 8"/20.5cm from beg or ¾"/2cm less than desired length ending with rnd 4 of rib pat. Work rnd 1 of rib pat 4 times. Bind off in pat.

Gauges

24 sts and 30 rnds to 4"/10cm over St st using size 5 (3.75mm) dpns. 24 sts and 30 rnds to 4"/10cm over modified Schiaparelli pat using size 5 (3.75mm) dpns. *Take time to check gauges.*

Textured Fingerless Mitts

THUMB
Transfer 13 thumb sts to dpns. Join yarn, pick up and k 2 sts, k 12 sts, k2tog (last thumb st and first picked-up st).
Next rnd K2tog, k around (13 sts). K 4 rnds. Bind off pwise.

Mitt 2
Work as for mitt 1, working thumb gusset as foll:
Set-up rnd K2, pm, p2, work rnd 2 of modified Schiaparelli pat over 20 sts, work rnd 4 of rib over 20 sts.

Finishing
Weave in ends. ■

Quick Tip
These versatile mitts can be worn with either the rib pattern (left) or the modified Schiaparelli pattern (right) as the palm.

156

Juliet Cap

Wear this feminine cap while out courting with your Romeo. An I-cord stem worked after the crown is knit tops off this dainty topper.

DESIGNED BY MARY SCOTT HUFF

Size
Instructions are written for one size.

Knitted Measurements
Head circumference 21½"/54.5cm
Depth 6½"/16.5cm

Materials
■ 1 1¾oz/50g hank (each approx 164yd/150m) of *Cascade 220 Sport* (Peruvian highland wool) in #8906 blue topaz

■ Size 4 (3.5mm) circular needle, 16"/40cm long *or size to obtain gauge*

■ One set (5) size 4 (3.5mm) double-pointed needles (dpns)

■ Stitch marker

Note
To work in the rnd, always read charts from right to left.

Stitch Glossary
Make bobble (MB) Work [k1, p1] twice in next st, turn; p4, turn; k4, turn; p4, turn; pass 2nd st over first, 3rd st over first, then 4th st over first st; sl this st to RH needle.

Hat
With circular needle, cast on 180 sts. Join and pm, taking care not to twist sts on needle.

BEG CHART PAT I
Rnd 1 Work 12-st rep 15 times. Cont to foll chart in this way to rnd 2—150 sts. Knit next rnd.

Gauge
28 sts and 36 rnds to 4"/10cm over chart pat II using size 4 (3.5mm) circular needle. *Take time to check gauge.*

Juliet Cap

BEG CHART PAT II
Rnd 1 Work 10-st rep 15 times. Cont to foll chart in this way to rnd 32.

CROWN SHAPING
Change to dpns (dividing sts evenly between 4 needles) when there are too few sts on circular needle.
Beg with rnd 33, cont to foll chart to rnd 45—30 sts. Knit next rnd.
Next (dec) rnd [K2tog] 15 times—15 sts. Knit next rnd.
Next (dec) rnd [K2tog] 6 times, k3tog—7 sts. Knit next rnd.
Next (dec) rnd [K2tog] 3 times, k1—4 sts.

I-CORD ACCENT
*Next row (RS) With 2nd dpn, k4, *do not turn.* Slide sts back to beg of needle to work next row from RS; rep from * five times more. Cut yarn leaving a 6"/15cm tail and thread through rem sts. Pull tog tightly and secure end. ■

CHART I

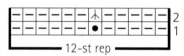

12-st rep

CHART II

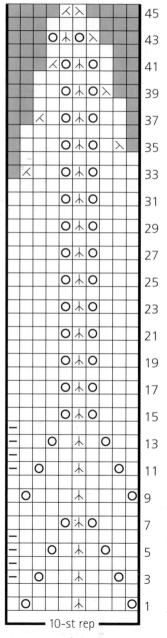

10-st rep

Stitch Key

□	Knit
−	Purl
O	Yarn over
⟋	K2tog
⟍	Ssk
⋏	SK2P
•	MB (Make Bobble)
▨	No stitch

158

Ribbed Newsboy Cap

Extra, extra! Read all about it! This jaunty, all-over ribbed unisex cap with attached brim is knit up double thick by holding two strands of yarn together.

DESIGNED BY YOKO HATTA

Size
Instructions are written for one size.

Knitted Measurements
Head circumference 21½"/54.5cm

Materials
- 2 1¾oz/50g hanks (each approx 164yd/150m) of *Cascade 220 Sport* (Peruvian highland wool) in #8622 camel
- One set (5) size 9 (5.5mm) double-pointed needles (dpns) *or size to obtain gauge*
- One pair size 8 (5mm) needles
- Stitch marker
- Two 1"/2.5cm buttons

Cap
With 2 strands of yarn held tog and larger needles, cast on 86 sts. Join and pm, taking care not to twist sts on needle.
Rnd 1 [*(K1, p2) 3 times, k1, p3; rep from * 3 times, k1, p3] twice.
Rnds 2–4 Work even in pat.
Rnd 5 [*K1, M1, p2, (k1, p2) 2 times, k1, p3; rep from * 3 times, k1, p3] twice—92 sts. **Rnds 6–7** Work even in pat. **Rnd 8** [*K1, p3, k1, M1, p2, k1, p2, k1, p3; rep from * 3 times, k1, p3]

twice—98 sts. **Rnd 9** Work even in pat.
Rnd 10 [*(K1, p3) 2 times, k1, M1, p2, k1, p3; rep from * 3 times, k1, p3] twice—104 sts. Cont in k1, p3 rib for 10 rnds more.

SHAPE CROWN
Rnd 1 [*(K1, p3) 3 times, k1, p1, p2tog; rep from * 3 times, k1, p1, p2tog] twice—96 sts.
Rnd 2 and all even rnds Work even in pat.
Rnd 3 [*(K1, p3) 2 times, k1, p1, p2tog, k1, p2; rep from * 3 times, k1, p2] twice—90 sts.
Rnd 5 [*K1, p3, k1, p1, p2tog, (k1, p2) 2 times; rep from * 3 times, k1, p2] twice—84 sts.

Rnd 7 [*K1, p1, p2tog, (k1, p2) 3 times; rep from * 3 times, k1, p2] twice—78 sts.
Rnd 9 [*(K1, p2) 3 times, k1, p2tog; rep from * 3 times, k1, p2tog] twice—70 sts.
Rnd 11 [*(K1, p2) 2 times, k1, p2tog, k1, p1; rep from * 3 times, k1, p1] twice—64 sts.
Rnd 13 [*K1, p2, k1, p2tog, (k1, p1) 2 times; rep from * 3 times, k1, p1] twice—58 sts.
Rnd 15 [*K1, p2tog, (k1, p1) 3 times; rep from * 3 times, k1, p1] twice—52 sts.
Rnd 17 [*(K1, p1) 3 times, k2tog; rep from * 3 times, k2tog] twice—44 sts.
Rnd 19 [*(K1, p1) 2 times, k2tog, k1; rep from * 3 times, k1] twice—38 sts.
Rnd 21 [*(K2tog) 2 times, k1; rep from * 3 times, k2tog, k2] twice—24 sts.
Rnd 22 *K2tog; rep from * around—12 sts. Cut yarn leaving an 8"/20.5cm tail and thread through rem sts. Pull tog tightly and secure end.

BRIM
With 2 strands held tog and smaller needles, cast on 54 sts. Work in garter st (knit every row) for 18 rows. Bind off.

Finishing
Block piece lightly to measurements. Sew brim to front edge of hat. Fold up corners of brim and tack to body of hat. Sew buttons on folded corners. ■

Gauge
16 sts and 19 rows to 4"/10cm over rib pat with 2 strands held tog using size 9 (5.5mm) needles. *Take time to check gauge.*

Chevron-Striped Beanie

This dapper hat gets its jaunty look from an easy-to-work chevron stitch knit in two alternating colors. It's finished with an I-cord knot on top.

DESIGNED BY CAROL J. SULCOSKI

Size
One size fits most adult women.

Knitted Measurements
Head circumference 19"/48cm
Depth 7"/18cm

Materials
- 1 1¾ oz/50g hank (each approx 164yd/150m) of *Cascade 220 Sport* (Peruvian highland wool) each in #4002 jet (MC) and #9404 ruby (CC)
- Size 6 (4mm) circular needle, 16"/40cm length *or size to obtain gauge*
- One set size 6 (4mm) double-pointed needles (dpns) *or size to obtain gauge*
- Stitch marker

Note
Change to dpns when there are too many sts to fit comfortably on circular needle.

Chevron St Pattern
(multiple of 15 sts)
Rnd 1 *K1, yo, k5, k3tog, k5, yo, k1; rep from * to end.
Rnd 2 Knit.
Rnd 3 Knit.
Rnd 4 Purl.

Beanie
Using circular needle and CC, cast on 105 sts. Join, taking care not to twist sts on needles, pm for beg of rnd.
Rnd 1 Knit.
Rnd 2 Purl.
Work one rep (four rnds) of chevron st pat.
Switch to MC and work one rep of chevron st pat.
Cont alternating CC and MC, working one rep of chevron st pat with each, until there are 4 bands of CC, and ending with CC.
Switch to MC and K 3 rnds.

SHAPE TOP
Dec rnd *K19, k2tog; rep from * to end.
Next rnd Knit.
Rep these 2 rnds 10 times more, knitting one less st before the dec on each subsequent dec rnd—50 sts.
Work dec rnd only, until 10 sts rem.
Next rnd K2tog; rep to end (5 sts).
Switch to CC, and knit I-cord that is approx 3.5"/9cm. Break off yarn and pass through rem sts. Weave in all ends, then tie a knot halfway down I-cord. ■

Gauge
22 sts/28 rnds = 4"/10cm over St st using size 6 (4mm) needle. *Take time to check gauge.*

56

Houndstooth Scarf

Channel your inner Brit in this traditional houndstooth scarf. With just two simple chart patterns to follow, it's an exemplary choice for first-time colorwork knitters!

DESIGNED BY LYNN M. WILSON

Size
Instructions are written for one size.

Knitted Measurements
Approx 7" x 54"/18cm x 137cm

Materials
■ 2 1¾oz/50g hanks (each approx 164yd/150m) of *Cascade 220 Sport* (Peruvian highland wool) each in #8893 hunter green (A) and #9421 blue hawaii (B)

■ One pair size 5 (3.75mm) needles *or size to obtain gauge*

■ Stitch markers

Scarf
With A, cast on 39 sts. Cont in St st for 7 rows, end with a RS row. Knit next row.

BEG CHART PAT I
Row 1 (RS) With A, k3, pm, work first st of chart, work 4-st rep 8 times, pm, with A, k3. Keeping 3 sts each side in garter st (knit every row), cont to foll chart in this way to row 6.

GARTER ST RIDGE I
With A, knit next 2 rows, inc 1 st in center of first row—40 sts.

BEG CHART PAT II
Row 1 (RS) With A, k3, sl marker, work first st of chart, work 8-st rep 4 times, work last st of chart, sl marker, with A, k3. Keeping 3 sts each side in garter st, cont to foll chart in this way to row 8, then rep rows 1–8 seven times more.

GARTER ST RIDGE II
Row 1 (RS) With A, knit.
Row 2 With A, purl.
Rows 3 and 4 With A, knit, dec 1 st in center of row 3—39 sts.

BEG CHART PAT I
Work same as above.

GARTER ST RIDGE I
Work same as above—40 sts.

BEG CHART PAT II
Work same as above, rep rows 1–8 three times more.

GARTER ST RIDGE II
Work same as above—39 sts.

BEG CHART PAT I
Work same as above.

GARTER ST RIDGE I
Work same as above—40 sts.

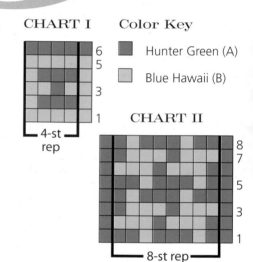

CHART I

6
5
3
1

4-st rep

Color Key

■ Hunter Green (A)

■ Blue Hawaii (B)

CHART II

8
7
5
3
1

8-st rep

BEG CHART PAT II
Work same as above, rep rows 1–8 seven times more.

GARTER ST RIDGE II
Work same as above—39 sts.**
Rep from ** to ** once more.

BEG CHART PAT I
Work same as above. With A, knit next 2 rows dropping markers. With A, cont in St st for 7 rows. Bind off purlwise.

FINISHING
Block piece to measurements. ■

Gauge
23 sts and 24 rows to 4"/10cm over St st and chart pats using size 5 (3.75mm) needles.
Take time to check gauge.

57

Fair Isle Tube Scarf

This totally tubular Nordic-inspired scarf is worked entirely in the round, making for a fun and cozy knit. Crochet-chain drawstrings topped with pompoms complete this classic look.

DESIGNED BY CHERYL MURRAY

Size

Instructions are written for one size.

Knitted Measurements

Approx 6½" x 58"/16.5cm x 147.5cm (excluding pompoms)

Materials

■ 3 1¾oz/50g hanks (each approx 164yd/150m) of *Cascade 220 Sport* (Peruvian highland wool) in #8010 natural (A)

■ 2 hanks in #8895 Christmas red (B)

■ 1 hank in #8885 dark plum (C)

■ Sizes 5 and 6 (3.75 and 4mm) circular needles, 16"/40cm long *or size to obtain gauge*

■ Size G/4 (4mm) crochet hook

■ 3"/7.5cm pompom maker

Notes

1) Scarf is worked in the round forming a tube.
2) To work in the round, always read chart from right to left.

Scarf

With smaller needle and A, cast on 88 sts loosely. Join and pm, taking care not to twist sts on needle.
Next rnd K44 (front sts), pm, k44 (back sts). Cont in St st (knit every rnd) for 3 rnds. Change to larger needle.
Next (turning ridge and eyelets) rnd P20, [yo, p2tog] twice, purl to end. Cont in St st as foll:

BEG CHART PAT

Rnd 1 Work first 44 sts for front, then last 44 sts for back. Cont to foll chart in this way to rnd 46, then rep rnds 5–46 nine times more, rnds 5–29 once, then rnds 1–4 once.
Next (turning ridge and eyelets) rnd P20, [yo, p2tog] twice, purl to end. Change to smaller needle. Cont in St st for 4 rnds. Bind off all sts loosely knitwise.

Finishing

Fold each end to WS along turning ridge and sew in place forming a casing. Flatten tube, centering front over back. Block to measurements.

DRAWSTRINGS (MAKE 2)

With crochet hook and A and B held tog, make a chain 12"/30.5cm long. Fasten off.
Thread each drawstring through a casing. Pull drawstring tightly to gather in and to close end of tube; knot securely.

POMPOMS (MAKE 2)

Using equal amounts of all 3 colors, wrap yarn densely around a 3"/7.5cm pompom maker. Finish pompom following package directions. Attach a pompom to the knot of a drawstring on each end. ■

Gauge

28 sts and 32 rnds to 4"/10cm over St st and chart pat using larger circular needle.
Take time to check gauge.

Fair Isle Tube Scarf

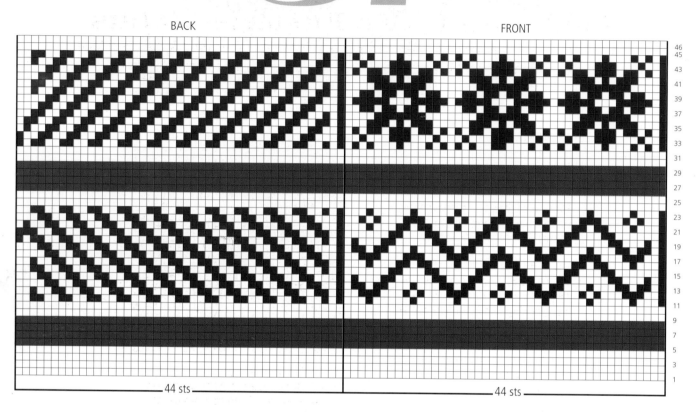

Color Key

☐ Natural (A)

■ Christmas Red (B)

■ Dark Plum (C)

Cables and Lace Fingerless Mitts

Flirty and ultra-feminine, these fingerless mitts feature columns of cables and lace and picot edgings. Wear them to dress up your most basic winter coat.

DESIGNED BY GRACE AKHREM

Size
Instructions are written for one size.

Knitted Measurements
Hand circumference 7"/18cm
Length Approx 8"/20.5cm

Materials
■ 1 1¾ oz/50g hank (each approx 164yd/150m) of *Cascade 220 Sport* (Peruvian highland wool) in #8401 silver grey
■ One set (5) size 3 (3.25mm) double-pointed needles (dpns) *or size to obtain gauge*
■ Cable needle (cn)
■ Stitch markers

Note
To work in the rnd, always read chart from right to left.

Stitch Glossary
2-st RT K2tog leaving sts on LH needle, k first st again, sl both sts from needle.
2-st LT With RH needle behind LH needle, skip the first st and k 2nd st tbl, insert RH needle into backs of both sts, k2tog tbl.
4-st RC Sl 2 sts to cn and hold to *back*, k2, k2 from cn.
4-st LC Sl 2 sts to cn and hold to *front*, k2, k2 from cn.

Right Mitt
Cast on 46 sts. Divide sts over 4 needles. Join, taking care not to twist sts on needles, pm for beg of rnds. Cont in picot hem as foll:

Gauge
26 sts and 32 rnds to 4"/10cm over St st and chart pat using size 3 (3.25mm) dpns.
Take time to check gauge.

Cables and Lace Fingerless Mitts

Stitch Key

☐	Knit
⊟	Purl
◎	Yarn over
⟋	K2tog
⟍	Ssk
⧖	2-st RT
⧗	2-st LT
⧗	4-st RC
⧗	4-st LC

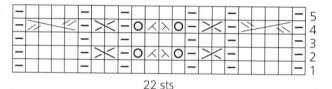

22 sts

Rnds 1–3 Knit.
Rnd (picot) 4 *Yo, k2tog;
rep from * around.
Rnds 5–7 Knit.

BEG CHART PAT
Rnd 1 K12, pm, work 22 sts of chart,
pm, k12. Keeping 12 sts each side of
chart in St st, cont to foll chart in

this way to rnd 5, then rep rnds 2–5 ten
times more.

THUMB PLACEMENT
Next rnd K12, sl marker, work rnd 2 of
chart, sl marker, k2, k8 onto waste yarn,
sl these 8 sts back to LH needle; knit
these 8 sts again, knit to end of rnd.
Work rnds 3–5 once, then rep rnds 2–5
three more times, then rnds 2 and 3
once. Rep rnds 1–7 of picot hem. Bind
off knitwise.

THUMB
Remove waste yarn and place 16 live sts
on dpns as foll: 8 sts below thumb
opening on needle 1 and 8 sts above
opening on needle 3. Join yarn, then k 8
sts on needle 1; with needle 2 pick up
and k 2 sts along side edge of opening; k
8 sts on needle 3; with needle 4 pick up
and k 2 sts along side edge of opening—
20 sts. Divide sts evenly between 4
needles. Join and pm for beg of rnds.
Knit 6 rnds. Bind off purlwise.

Left Mitt
Work same as right mitt to thumb
placement.

THUMB PLACEMENT
Next rnd K2, k8 onto waste yarn, sl
these 8 sts back to LH needle; knit these
8 sts again, k2, sl marker, work rnd 2 of
chart, sl marker, knit to end of rnd.
Cont to work same as right mitt.

Finishing
Turn top and bottom edges to WS
along picot rnd and hem in place.
Block to shape. ∎

59

Tasseled Fair Isle Scarf

Start your winter off in style in this vintage-style neck warmer. Colorwork, ribbing, tassels and a touch of garter stitch provide an abundance of techniques to try.

DESIGNED BY JACQUELINE VAN DILLEN

■■◀■▢

Size
Instructions are written for one size.

Knitted Measurements
Approx 6.25" x 71"/16cm x 180cm (excluding fringe)

Materials
■ 3 1¾oz/50g hanks (each approx 164yd/150m) of *Cascade 220 Sport* (Peruvian highland wool) in #8010 natural (MC)

■ 1 1¾oz/50g hank (each approx 164yd/150m) of *Cascade 220 Sport* (Peruvian highland wool) each in #8892 azure (A) and #8906 blue topaz (B)

■ One pair size 4 (3.5mm) needles *or size to obtain gauge*

■ Size E/4 (3.5mm) crochet hook

Stitch Glossary
FAKE PATENT ST
(multiple of 4 sts plus 2)
Row 1 (RS) Sl 1 * K2, p1, k1; rep from * to last st, k1.

Row 2 Sl 1, * K3, p1; rep from * to last st, p1.
Rep rows 1 and 2 for pattern stitch.

Scarf
With B, cast on 38 sts. Knit 2 rows. Work garter st stripes as foll: [Knit 2 rows A, knit 2 rows B] 3 times.

BEG CHART
Row 1 (RS) Sl 1 wyib, work 6-st chart rep 6 times across, k1 with last color worked. **Row 2** Sl 1 wyif, work 6-st chart rep 6 times across, p1. Cont to work chart in this manner until row 36 is complete.

BEG PAT ST
Work in fake patent st until piece measures 64½"/164cm from beg, end with a WS row.
REVERSE CHART
Next row (RS) Sl 1 wyib, work row 35 of chart, working 6-st rep 6 times across, k1. **Next row (WS)** Sl 1 wyif, work row 34 of chart, working 6-st rep 6 times across, p1. Cont to work chart in this manner until row 1 is complete. Work garter st stripes as foll: [Purl

2 rows B, purl 2 rows A] 3 times. Purl 2 rows B. Bind off with B.

Finishing
Block scarf to measurements.

CROCHET EDGING
With crochet hook, B and RS facing, join yarn with sl st at upper RH corner of scarf, ch 1, *sc into next edge st, sk 1, 4dc in next edge st (1 bow made), sk 1; rep from * once more. Switch to MC, *sc into next edge st, sk 1, 4dc into next edge st, sk 1; rep from * 71 times more. Switch to B, *sc, sk 1, 4dc, sk 1; rep from * once more, fasten off—76 bows. Repeat along other side.

FRINGE (MAKE 4)
With B, cut 16 strands each 8"/20.5cm long. Attach to corner of scarf with crochet hook. ■

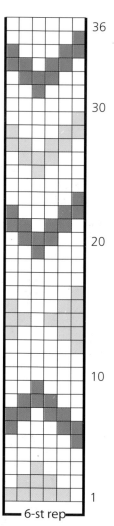

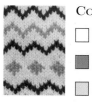

Color Key
□ Natural (MC)
▨ Azure (A)
▨ Blue Topaz (B)

6-st rep

Gauge
22 sts and 30 rows to 4"/10cm over fake patent st using size 4 (3.5mm) needles. *Take time to check gauge.*

Bobbled Gauntlets

Warm hands, warm heart! Cut the chill and keep your hands cozy with extra-long cuffs and fitted ribbing around the wrists. Cables, bobbles and a picot edging create a feminine touch.

DESIGNED BY CHERYL MURRAY

Size
Instructions are written for one size.

Knitted Measurements
Hand circumference 7½"/19cm
Length of cuff Approx 6½"/16.5cm

Materials
■ 2 1¾oz/50g hanks (each approx 164yd/150m) of *Cascade 220 Sport* (Peruvian highland wool) in #8895 Christmas red

■ One set (5) each sizes 4 and 5 (3.5 and 3.75mm) double-pointed needles (dpns) *or size to obtain gauge*

■ Cable needle (cn)

■ Stitch markers

Note
To work in the rnd, always read chart from right to left.

Stitch Glossary
3-st RPC Sl 1 st to cn and hold to *back*, k2, p1 from cn.
3-st LPC Sl 2 sts to cn and hold to *front*, p1, k2 from cn.
Make bobble (MB) [K in front and back of next st] twice, turn; p4, turn; k4, turn; [p2tog] twice, turn; k2tog.

Mitten (make 2)
CUFF
With smaller dpns, cast on 56 sts loosely. Divide sts over 4 needles. Join taking care not to twist sts on needles, pm for beg of rnds. Cont in St st (knit every rnd) for 4 rnds. Change to larger dpns.
Next (picot) rnd *P2tog, yo; rep from * around. Knit next rnd.

BEG CHART PAT
Rnd 1 Work 14-st rep 4 times. Cont to foll chart in this way to rnd 50—48 sts. Cont in rib pat as foll:
Next rnd *P2, k2; rep from * around. Rep this rnd 9 times more.
Knit next 2 rnds.

THUMB GUSSET
Inc rnd 1 M1, k2, M1, pm, knit to end of rnd—50 sts. Knit next 2 rnds.
Inc rnd 2 M1, knit to marker, M1, sl marker, knit to end of rnd—52 sts. Knit next 2 rnds. Rep last 3 rnds 5 times more—62 sts (16 sts between thumb gusset markers).
Next rnd Place first 16 sts on scrap yarn for thumb, drop marker, cast on 2 sts, knit to end of rnd—48 sts.

HAND
Work even in St st until piece measures 6"/15cm from last rnd of rib pat.

TOP SHAPING
Dec rnd 1 [K10, k2tog] 4 times—44 sts. Knit next rnd.
Dec rnd 2 [K9, k2tog] 4 times—40 sts. Knit next rnd.
Dec rnd 3 [K8, k2tog] 4 times—36 sts. Knit next rnd.
Dec rnd 4 [K7, k2tog] 4 times—32 sts. Knit next rnd.
Dec rnd 5 [K6, k2tog] 4 times—28 sts. Knit next rnd.

Gauge
26 sts and 36 rnds to 4"/10cm over St st using larger dpns. *Take time to check gauge.*

Dec rnd 6 [K5, k2tog] 4 times—24 sts. Knit next rnd.

Dec rnd 7 [K4, k2tog] 4 times—20 sts. Knit next rnd.

Dec rnd 8 [K3, k2tog] 4 times—16 sts. Knit next rnd.

Dec rnd 9 [K2, k2tog] 4 times—12 sts. Knit next rnd.

Dec rnd 10 [K1, k2tog] 4 times—8 sts. Cut yarn leaving an 8"/20.5cm tail and thread through rem sts. Pull tog tightly and secure end.

THUMB

Place 16 thumb gusset sts over 2 larger needles.

Next rnd Join yarn and knit across sts, then pick up and k 2 sts over cast-on of opening—18 sts. Divide sts evenly over 3 needles. Join and pm for beg of rnds. Cont in St st for 2"/5cm.

TOP SHAPING

Dec rnd 1 *K1, k2tog; rep from * around—12 sts.

Dec rnd 2 [K2tog] 6 times—6 sts. Cut yarn leaving a 6"/15cm tail and thread through rem sts. Pull tog tightly and secure end.

Finishing

Turn bottom edge of cuff to WS along picot rnd and hem in place. ■

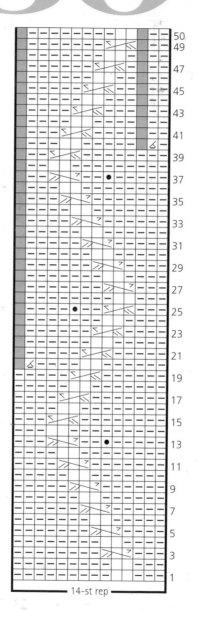

14-st rep

Stitch Key

- ☐ Knit
- ⊟ Purl
- ◲ P2tog
- ● Make Bobble
- ◥◤ 3-st-RPC
- ◤◢ 3-st LPC
- ▨ No stitch